PORTRAITS OF THE CIVIL WAR

PORTRAITS OF THE CIVIL WAR

WILLIAM C. DAVIS

SMITHMARK

This edition published in 1999 by SMITHMARK Publishers, a division of
U.S. Media Holdings, Inc.
115 West 18th Street, New York, NY 10011

SMITHMARK books are available for bulk purchase for sales promotion and premium
use. For details write or call the sales manager of special sales, SMITHMARK Publishers,
115 West 18th Street, New York, NY 10011.

Produced by Salamander Books
8 Blenheim Court
Brewery Road
London
N7 9NT

ISBN 0-7651-1691-X
10 9 8 7 6 5 4 3 2 1

CREDITS
Project managed by Ray Bonds
Designed by Megra Mitchell
Mono reproduction by Studio Technology Limited, Leeds
Printed in Italy

THE AUTHOR
William C. Davis has written more than 30 books on the Civil War period, including two
that have achieved Pulitzer Prize nominations. He has acted as a consultant and advisor to
many organizations and is a frequent lecturer on the subject.

PRELIM PHOTOGRAPHS

Page 1: A classic photograph, from the Mathew Brady Collection, of Abraham Lincoln,
16th president of the United States, at a camp at Antietam, in September 1862. He is
flanked by (left) detective Major Allen and (right) General Lew Wallace, who fought at
Shiloh and was regarded by many as having been appointed by Lincoln more for his
political influence than his military experience.

Page 3: Another photo from the Brady Collection, of Sherman at Atlanta, Georgia. He
was one of the greatest of all American soldiers, who following the war turned down many
requests to run for president.

Page 5: Confederate Captain (later Admiral and General) Raphael Semmes aboard
Alabama in Cape Town, South Africa, in August 1863. He and the *Alabama* terrorized
Northern shipping, capturing 55 prizes in 22 months before the ship was sunk by USS
Kearsarge off Cherbourg, France, in June 1864. In the background is Lieutenant J.M. Kell.

Page 7: Mathew Brady, most famed of all Civil War photographers, who seemed to have
captured the images of almost every battlefield of the war, yet most of the images credited
to him were in fact taken by assistants, for Brady was suffering with extremely poor sight
by the time America went to war with itself.

CONTENTS

INTRODUCTION

Two momentous events occurred coincidentally in 1861, to produce one of history's great synergies. An infant industry, photography, came of age, and America went to war with itself. The result was the first and still one of the greatest records ever created of an entire human experience, for when Johnny Reb and Billy Yank went to war, the camera went with them.

In fact, thousands of cameras went to war. Out of civilian studios all across the North and South, there poured hundreds of thousands of soldier portraits, and that many and more of those inhabiting the home front. Meanwhile, scores of artists went with the armies, recording the soldiers in the field, and the carnage of the battlefields just hours after the fighting ceased. The men—and a few women—behind those cameras had little idea of how long their images would last, or how important they would be in revealing to future generations, and centuries, the face of war.

As for the faces in front of the cameras, they were the very image of America, from rustic to aristocrat. Few could resist the allure or the novelty of seeing their visages fixed on glass or tin or paper. From generals and admirals, and presidents even, down to the lowliest private in the ranks, they all sought to leave their shadows in silver and albumen for themselves, those back home, and posterity. It was everyone's war in time, and in time everyone sat for the artists, white and black, male and female, Hispanic, Indian, and even the animals. Anyone and anything could be a subject. One photographer even took an image of a general's cigar.

In *Portraits of the Civil War* sixty of these faces will look you in the eye, and challenge you to see in them their stories and the trial through which they passed. They are the faces of officers who fought for freedom, of presidents who struggled for their countries, of the politicians who made war, and the common soldiers doomed to fight and die. There is heroism and folly and determination, and most of all sacrifice in their faces. Some achieved a brief glimmer of fame. Others made their names feared and revered for all time. All of them knew somehow that they were living out not only the greatest experience of their lives, but a defining moment for their people, and a few knew even that what they did would have an impact on the future of western civilization.

Of course they are all gone now, the photographers and the photographed. But they all enjoy a kind of immortality in their images left behind. Studying them, and learning their stories, we may find that despite the strange clothing and sometimes unconventional hair styles, they do not look so different from ourselves and those we know. Seeing and accepting that forces us to the chilling realization that anyone can find themselves forced to endure what they endured. Knowing that, we can only hope no one in future generations will open a book and find our faces staring out from the pages, testimony to a trial as great as that suffered by our Civil War ancestors. For these fading images are not just a record of the past. They are a warning as well. The bells that tolled for them and their generation are ringing still.

William C. Davis
Mechanicsburg
Pennsylvania
1999

TURNER ASHBY

Surely no Confederate cavalryman possessed more dash than Turner Ashby, Stonewall Jackson's trusted wizard in the saddle who helped him make the 1862 campaign in the Shenandoah Valley legendary.

Born in Fauquier County, Virginia, October 23, 1828, Ashby grew up with the martial spirit of a father who was an officer in the War of 1812, and a grandfather who held a commission in the Revolution. Privately educated by a local militia officer, young Ashby started out in life as a farmer, and seemingly took no part in the growing debate over slavery and secession in the late 1850s, though he did lead a militia company that went to Harpers Ferry in October 1859 to put down John Brown's raid. The main picture shows him as captain of the militia company, Ashby's Mountain Rangers. As late as 1860, like most Virginians, he was still attached to the Union and hoping for compromise, but when his state seceded in April 1861 he went with it into the Confederacy.

Ashby's militia company became initially a part of the 7th Virginia Cavalry, assigned to scouting and intelligence gathering in the northern Shenandoah, but he would see no real action until he was commissioned colonel commanding the regiment and attached to the command of rising star Major General Thomas J. "Stonewall" Jackson late in 1861. From then on for the brief remainder of his life, Ashby's fortunes were intertwined with the mighty Stonewall's.

Ashby led a regiment of cavalry in the outset of Jackson's operations in the Valley in March 1862, shadowing the Federals while Jackson set his plans to meet and defeat three Yankee armies in motion. Along the way the daring cavalryman harassed enemy movements, making swift attacks on flanks and outposts, to keep the Union commanders off guard. Ashby then joined Jackson's main army to fight at Winchester on May 25, and two days later was rewarded with promotion to brigadier general. The glory, however, did not last long. Ten days later, on June 6, while he and his command were covering Jackson's rear near Harrisonburg, his horse was cut down under him in a skirmish. Ashby got clear of the dead animal and led his men on foot, yelling at them "Charge, men; for God's sake, charge," when a bullet killed him almost instantly. The inset picture is the only known wartime photo of Ashby in uniform, ironically taken in death, probably on June 7 1862.

Ashby fell when his promise was yet bright for better things. "I never knew his superior," a shaken Jackson lamented. "His daring was proverbial." One of his men said simply, "He is the bravest man that I ever saw."

Henry A. Barnum

Incredibly, easily the most exhibitionist general of the Civil War coincidentally bore a name that was itself synonymous in the nineteenth century with rank exhibitionism, and it never seemed to occur to him.

Henry A. Barnum was a New Yorker, born in Jamesville in the western part of the state, September 24, 1833. Educated at the Syracuse Institute, he took up the law and at the same time became involved in local militia affairs on the eve of the outbreak of war. Thus, when the fighting began, he enlisted and was soon elected a captain in the 12th New York Infantry. He led his company in action for the first time in the battle at Manassas on July 21, his company standing its ground while the rest of the regiment fell back in disarray in the Union rout.

Barnum went on to fight again on the Virginia peninsula in the spring of 1862, and in the last of the Seven Days battles on July 1, at Malvern Hill, Barnum went down while leading a charge, with a painful, though not life-threatening wound, when a bullet penetrated his lower right hip and buttock. At first his men left him for dead on the field, and later a dead officer was mistaken for him and buried with Barnum's name on the headboard. But soon his men took Barnum from the field to the Malvern house itself to treat his wound. Confederates captured him there and sent him to a prison in Richmond, where he recuperated while awaiting exchange.

Returned to his army, he built the 149th New York and took command as its colonel, and thereafter fought with the Army of the Potomac at Gettysburg, and then was transferred west in the concentration of forces that lifted the siege of Chattanooga. In the Battle of Lookout Mountain Barnum took another wound, but went on to lead his regiment in the Atlanta Campaign, and a full brigade in Sherman's March to the Sea. With the war all but over, he was among the last men promoted to brigadier general, his commission dating May 31, 1865.

In an equally bizarre twist of fate, following the battle at Malvern Hill and his capture, Barnum later learned that another body found on the field had been mistakenly identified as his own. It was buried under a headstone with his name, and at his home town a military funeral mourned his passing. His death, like his habit of displaying his wound, was somewhat exaggerated. Barnum spent the rest of his life in minor public offices and working at veterans' affairs, but to posterity he will always be best known for his predilection for standing before the camera in full uniform and dignified poise, with his trousers down and a leather strap run through the old wound in his buttock. P. T. Barnum would have been proud of him.

CLARA BARTON

There are some achievements that require not only imagination, but also an indomitable determination in the face of odds and opposition. Clara Barton knew all about that, but thanks to her persistence the world has been the beneficiary.

Women, of course, were not supposed to have a role in this war, other than urging young men to enlist. For Clara Barton, born Christmas day, 1821, a lifetime spent as a school teacher seemed to offer nothing to the Union cause in 1861 when she was forty. She was working at the Patent Office in Washington in April when she saw her first soldiers, the 6th Massachusetts, which had been attacked by a pro-Southern mob in Baltimore on its way to the capital. Many of the men were injured, and Barton spontaneously organized some local women into a relief group to see to their nursing and comfort.

That commenced her true calling. The aftermath of the first battle at Bull Run in July revealed that the military was wholly unprepared for the care of the wounded, especially in the way of supplies. The whole Union army had only eleven thermometers! She once more organized a relief charitable organization, this time on a much larger scale, and soon had the sanction of the surgeon general for her efforts. By 1862 she was actually traveling with the Army of the Potomac on an official pass, and thereafter spent the rest of the war alternately raising money and donations of supplies, and tending soldiers in the field, from Washington to South Carolina, wherever the eastern armies went. In 1864 she was made superintendent of nurses in the Army of the James, and before the war ended was already busy at the work of helping families locate missing sons, and later in marking the graves of the dead at Andersonville.

The experience she gained in the Civil War put Barton on the path she would follow for the rest of her life. Twenty years after she tended those first injured Massachusetts soldiers, she finally founded the American Red Cross in 1881, and thereafter served as its head until 1904. When she died April 12, 1912, she had become internationally famed as a humanitarian, and had her organization in place and ready, this time, for the coming wars of the twentieth century, as well as the myriad civil endeavors that have seen the organization she started spread around the globe.

P. G.T. Beauregard

They liked to call him the "Napoleon in Gray," and he liked it when they called him that. No general of the Confederacy began the war with brighter promise, yet few at the end had been dogged by more controversy and acrimony, or unrealized potential.

He was born on a Creole in St. Bernard Parish, below New Orleans, on May 28, 1818. Pierre Gustave Toutant Beauregard grew up studying Napoleon, which attracted him to a military career, for which his appointment to the United States Military Academy at West Point was a natural first step. He was an excellent cadet, finishing second in his class in 1838, and would spend the next 23 years in the army. In the war with Mexico, he performed brilliantly in the battles at Contreras and Churubusco and finally at Chapultepec, then spent the 1850s in routine engineer duty before being assigned superintendent at West Point in January 1861, three days before his native Louisiana seceded.

He held the post a mere two days, then resigned his commission in February and went south to the new Confederate capital at Montgomery, Alabama. He immediately secured a commission as brigadier general and assignment to Charleston to deal with Fort Sumter. On April 12, 1861, his batteries began the war when they opened fire, and the subsequent surrender of the fort made Beauregard the South's first military hero. He followed this with a shared victory with Joseph E. Johnston in the first Battle of Manassas on July 21 that won him promotion to the highest rank of general and the adulation of the new nation.

But then the problems began. Beauregard was haughty and proud. He clashed with President Davis, and initial disagreements soon turned into outright enmity on both parts. At his own request Beauregard was reassigned from the Virginia theater, and became Albert Sidney Johnston's second in command in the campaign that led to the April 6-7, 1862 Battle of Shiloh. When Johnston was killed the first day, Beauregard assumed command, but failed to follow up his initial advantage, and retreated. Reassigned to Charleston again, he repelled Union land and naval assaults in the spring of 1863, and the next year commanded in North Carolina and southern Virginia, where he probably saved Petersburg and Richmond from capture by Grant. But his feud with Davis ensured that he never held a major field command again.

After the war Beauregard turned to railroading, and supervised the Louisiana lottery, but his real passion was his continuing feud with Davis, which he fought out in the pages of his partisan and contentious memoirs. His death on February 20, 1893, did not end the controversy over his capabilities.

BELLE BOYD

To later generations the unbridled and often seemingly comic opera romanticism of the Civil War era can seem almost silly, but to the people at the time it was very serious, indeed. If they actually achieved or contributed very little, their adventures were none the less captivating to their generation.

Scores of young girls set out to be spies. Best known of all, and among the more useful, was Belle Boyd, a seventeen-year-old Virginia girl when the war broke out. Her home town Martinsburg—now in West Virginia—was occupied by the Federals early in the conflict and remained in Union hands for most of the war.

When a Yankee soldier entered her home on the Fourth of July in 1861, she took a pistol and shot at him to drive him away, but thereafter changed her tack and tried to charm information out of Union officers. Belle was no beauty, but she had an undeniably winning personality, and she occasionally learned enough to send via couriers to Confederates lurking in the vicinity. Late in 1861 she apparently rode as a courier herself on occasion, and a few months later was arrested by Union authorities who suspected her, but she was soon released. Confederate cavalryman Turner Ashby was a special recipient of information from her, and on May 23, 1862, during Stonewall Jackson's fabled Shenandoah Campaign, she ran on foot to meet Jackson's troops as they neared Front Royal, to give the general vital information of enemy troops and dispositions. She actually came under fire during her sprint, but escaped unharmed.

Moreover, it made her a national celebrity in the Confederacy, only for her to get her arrested and imprisoned once more. When she was released, the authorities deported her across the lines to Richmond, where she was received as a heroine and made an honorary aide on Jackson's staff. Returning to Martinsburg, she was arrested and deported once more, and finally went to England on a blockade runner, only to be captured. Eventually she married the captain of the Yankee ship that captured her, but it did not save her from one last brief arrest in the winter of 1864-65.

Belle Boyd Hardinge wrote a lurid and exaggerated memoir of her adventures while in England, and after her husband died in 1866 she took to the stage giving dramatic lectures based on her now highly fictionalized exploits. Twice more she married, and continued on the stage intermittently almost until the end of the century. She died in Wisconsin in 1900, having so confused her actual career with fabrications and exaggerations that what she really did and did not do during the war may never accurately be known.

MATHEW BRADY

Seldom in history has an artist so dominated his field that his very name became synonymous with the product of his art, but it happened during the Civil War, when everyone knew without mistake what was meant when a man said he "went for his Brady."

Photography was well into its second generation when the war began. It had come to America in 1839 in the process invented by Louis Daguerre of France. Mathew Brady, born in New York around 1823, was early attracted to this new art form and, when only in his twenties, acquired a dramatic proficiency as a daguerrian artist. Keeping abreast of the rapidly developing technology, Brady mastered more modern techniques and, blending them with his undeniable skill with the camera, was soon the most noted photographer in the country, his studios in New York and Washington becoming the stopping places of leaders in politics, the arts, and society.

Brady combined an instinct for entrepreneurism with a sure eye for spotting talent in younger photographers, and both came together for him in 1861 when the country went to war. Immediately Brady sensed an opportunity to be the first to capture warfare on camera in all its facets. "A spirit in my feet said 'go'," he would say, "and I went." Well known to leading military and political figures, Brady had no trouble getting passes for himself and his staff to accompany the armies. Brady himself took his field darkroom to the first Battle of Bull Run, though none of his images taken there has survived. But thereafter there were few battlefields east of the Appalachians that did not have a Brady camera capturing the scenes of carnage.

Ironically, Brady himself by wartime was so nearsighted that he may not have been able to focus a camera outside his studio. All or most of his war photos were thus taken by assistants like Alexander Gardner and Timothy O'Sullivan, themselves pioneering artists, yet Brady craftily allowed the public to think all of his images were "by Brady," thus spreading his reputation. He hoped to amass a priceless archive of images, and indeed he did, nearly 6,000 of them, but after the war he found no market for them. By 1875 he was almost bankrupt and forced to sell the collection to the government for a mere $25,000, a fraction of his investment. He died almost a pauper on January 16, 1896, just as advances in printing technology were about to realize his dream by bringing his photographs to the world.

Photo taken July 22d 1861

BRADY The Photograph returned ...

BRAXTON BRAGG

One of his subordinate generals threatened to slap his face and force him to fight. Others plotted against him, and there were even stories that in the war with Mexico one of his men tried to assassinate him. Needless to say, Braxton Bragg was not a popular man.

This most controversial of future Confederate chieftains was born March 22, 1817, in North Carolina, and graduated high in his class at West Point in 1837, when he went into the artillery. After service against the Seminoles in Florida, he went into the Mexican conflict as a captain serving under General Zachary Taylor. Bragg and his battery performed excellently at the Battle of Buena Vista where he was instrumental in the victory, and Taylor's expression "a little more grape, Captain Bragg" made him something of a household name. But he also had a reputation for being contentious, and in 1856 he left the army to become a Louisiana sugar planter.

When Louisiana seceded in January 1861, Bragg led the state militia that seized the Federal arsenal at Baton Rouge, and soon after President Davis made him a brigadier general and sent him to Pensacola, Florida. The first year of the war passed him by, however, until he was called to northern Mississippi by Albert Sidney Johnston as he built an army to drive the Yankees out of west Tennessee and Kentucky. Bragg commanded a corps under Johnston in the Battle of Shiloh and fought well, winning promotion to full rank general, and in June 1862 he took command of the Army of Tennessee after Davis relieved the out-of-favor Beauregard.

In the fall of 1862 he led his army into Kentucky and was initially successful before being forced out of the state again. He fought again at Stones River in middle Tennessee, and was forced to retire, but he came back in September to fight and win the Battle of Chickamauga, the most decisive field victory the Army of Tennessee would ever win. Bragg lost its benefits when he failed to pursue the beaten foe vigorously. Instead he besieged the Federals at Chattanooga, but was driven off in a disastrous rout by newly arrived U. S. Grant in November. Disgraced, Bragg had no choice but to resign

Davis, who always felt a fondness and trust for Bragg, made him his military advisor through most of 1864, and then in 1865 Bragg again held small commands in North Carolina until the war's end. He turned to engineering after the war, but on September 27, 1876, fell dead in the street at Galveston. Few who served under him would mourn his passing.

JOHN C. BRECKINRIDGE

To some, he was the ideal of a Kentucky gentleman. Tall, handsome, a superb horseman, eloquent orator, and fearless commander, he represented everything that mid-nineteenth century men aspired to be. Yet to others he was the worst sort of traitor.

John Cabell Breckinridge was born January 16, 1821, in Lexington, Kentucky, to one of the most distinguished families in the Bluegrass, his grandfather having been Thomas Jefferson's attorney general. He attended Centre College, then Princeton briefly, and finally Transylvania University, and set out on a career in the law. When war came with Mexico, he volunteered and was elected major of the 3d Kentucky Infantry, which he helped lead to Mexico City, though he saw no action.

Politics beckoned on his return, and even though he was a Democrat in a heavily Whig region, he won a seat in the legislature, and in 1851 was elected to Congress for the first of two terms. In 1855 he turned down the territorial governorship of Washington, but the next year the Democrats nominated him as James Buchanan's running mate. At his election in 1856, Breckinridge, still only 35, was the youngest vice president in American history. Always a moderate on the slavery and state rights issues, he was nominated for the presidency in 1860 by the Southern wing of his party, and placed second to Lincoln in the electoral ballot.

Breckinridge was serving as a senator from Kentucky when the war started, and tried to remain loyal, but finally fled to the Confederacy when his arrest was ordered by Federals suspicious of his sympathies. President Davis immediately made him a brigadier general, and though he had never led men in combat Breckinridge took command of the reserve corps in the army that fought at Shiloh. Thereafter he learned the military craft quickly, fighting with distinction at Baton Rouge, Vicksburg, Stones River, and especially at Chickamauga. He and his army commander Braxton Bragg did not get along, however, and after Breckinridge's corps collapsed on Missionary Ridge in November 1863 he was reassigned to Virginia.

On May 15, 1864, Breckinridge, against superior enemy numbers, fought one of the most dramatic small battles of the war at New Market, and thereafter commanded ably in western Virginia until February 1865 when Davis made him secretary of war. Breckinridge oversaw the flight of the Confederate government in April-May, and himself made a dramatic escape through Florida and across the Gulf to Cuba in an open boat. He lived in England and Canada in exile until 1868, then returned to Kentucky and stood thereafter for amity and reconciliation between the sections. He died May 17, 1875, universally esteemed to the North and South.

FRANCIS BROWNELL

In those dark days of April and May 1861, the Union cause desperately needed some heroes. The humiliation of the fall of Fort Sumter, the capture of arsenals and Federal offices all across the seceding South, cast a gloom over Washington only made worse by its geographical exposure, with Virginia and a growing Confederate army just across the Potomac. In a moment of tragedy, the North got its hero.

When Abraham Lincoln took office as president, one of his very first acts was to ensure the commissioning of young E. Elmer Ellsworth, who just the year before briefly studied law in Lincoln's Illinois office. Ellsworth had raised his own regiment from among members of New York City's fire departments, and now as a colonel he commanded them as the 11th New York Fire Zouaves. One of them was Private Francis Edwin Brownell, a New Yorker who had only enlisted on April 20. On May 7 Brownell was mustered into the army for a two-year hitch when Ellsworth and his regiment came to Washington. Brownell and his comrades were a rowdy bunch, not surprising given the reputation of New York's firemen, but they were also a blessing when they helped extinguish a dangerous fire in the Capitol.

It fell to Brownell and the rest of Ellsworth's regiment to be the first to take the Stars and Stripes back across the Potomac. On the early misty morning of May 24, the 11th New York made a quick crossing of the river and marched up the main street of Alexandria, just in time to see the remnants of a small Confederate contingent evacuating the town. For some time the firemen marched the city streets, making certain their position was secure. Brownell himself stayed with Ellsworth, and was with him when they saw a secession flag still flying from the roof of the Marshall House hotel, clearly left there to defy them.

Ellsworth and Brownell marched into the hotel, right past proprietor James T. Jackson, and climbed the stairs to step out on the roof and tear down the flag. As they descended, Jackson appeared with a shotgun and aimed it at Brownell. The private jumped at him, attempting to turn the gun aside, but it went off and hit Ellsworth full in the chest without warning, killing him instantly. Brownell immediately emptied his musket into Jackson and then finished killing him with his bayonet.

Ellsworth became the Union's first martyr, and that made his avenger Brownell its first hero. Brownell retrieved the bloodstained flag from Ellsworth, and thereafter posed for photographers with the banner beneath his heel. He was immediately commissioned a lieutenant, and thereafter saw action at Bull Run and elsewhere before he mustered out in 1863. In 1877 he received his final recognition for killing Jackson when he was awarded the Medal of Honor.

AMBROSE EVERETT BURNSIDE

Years after his birth there were stories that on first leaving his mother's womb, he refused to breathe. A doctor had to take a feather and tickle his nose until a sneeze started his lungs working. True or not, it spoke volumes about a man who almost destroyed his army, but left his whiskers as a permanent part of western culture.

Feather or no, he was born Ambrose Everett Burnside at Liberty, Indiana, May 24, 1824, the son of a South Carolina slave owner who had emancipated his slaves and moved north. Burnside started out apprenticed to the tailoring trade, but political connections got him an appointment to West Point in 1843, and four years later he graduated high enough to get a commission in the artillery. Burnside spent the next five years mostly on frontier duty in the southwest, but resigned in 1853 to go into business in Rhode Island, having invented and patented a new pattern of breech-loading rifle that he hoped to sell to the army. The Burnside Carbine was an excellent weapon, but the army then was mired in a muzzle-loading peacetime mindset.

In 1861 Burnside immediately raised the 1st Rhode Island and led it to Washington, where he was commissioned a colonel and commanded a brigade in the debacle at First Manassas. Lincoln made him a brigadier general in August, and sent him to secure a foothold on the North Carolina coast for future penetrations of the Confederate interior. Burnside did well, getting a second star in return, and in July 1862 joined his old friend McClellan's Army of the Potomac. He failed to perform very aggressively or imaginatively at Antietam, where he left his name on a bridge that he absorbed horrible casualties in taking, but when Lincoln relieved McClellan in November, Burnside got the command of the army, despite having reputedly turned it down twice before.

When he did act at Fredricksburg in December, it was disastrously. Having planned a brilliant campaign, logistics beyond his control let him down, but he unimaginatively pressed on, piling up casualties in senseless attacks. A bungled campaign soon followed in the Virginia winter mud that exhausted his army and achieved nothing, and Lincoln relieved him of command in March, sending him west. Burnside's military star never rose again, despite an able defense of Knoxville in the fall of 1863. In 1864 he commanded a corps in the Petersburg siege, but finally resigned in April 1865. Yet he remained popular at home, and would serve several terms as governor of Rhode Island and one term as a senator, dying September 13, 1881. Ironically, he is best remembered for something even his own frequent indecisiveness could not stop—his whiskers. He grew flamboyant mutton-chops that attracted so much attention that they were called "burnsides," soon turned around to become "sideburns," a ticklishly fitting memorial for a man who had to be tickled into living.

MARY BOYKIN CHESNUT

Some people are destined to be remembered chiefly for what they did that allows us to recall those around them. By being in exactly the right place and at the right time, Mary Boykin Chesnut gave us a window into the heart of the Southern cause through her matchless journal. She was truly the diarist of the Confederacy.

She was born March 31, 1823, as Mary Boykin Miller, the daughter of a governor of South Carolina, and a member of the small oligarchy of prominent families who ruled the Palmetto State. She enjoyed all the benefits of education and privilege of her class, and then in 1840 married James Chesnut, Jr., himself the son of a prominent family, and a practicing attorney in Camden. As her husband rose in politics, Mary Chesnut saw her circle of acquaintance and experience widen to include the state capital, and later in 1858 moved to Washington when her husband took a seat in the United States Senate. The social world of the national capital was her rehearsal for another capital to come. When Chesnut resigned after South Carolina's secession, and was sent as a delegate to the convention in Montgomery, Alabama, which created the Confederate government, she went with him.

Shortly before going to Montgomery, Mary began sporadically keeping a journal, but soon undertook making extended records of her observations of men and women and events on a daily basis. Well acquainted with President Jefferson Davis and most of the other Confederate leaders, she quickly made her expanding diary the pre-eminent record of the inner life of the new nation, especially benefiting her husband's vantage as a congressman, then an officer on General Beauregard's staff, and finally as a general and aide to Davis himself. After witnessing the formation of the new government, she was in Charleston to observe the bombardment of Fort Sumter, and thereafter went to the new capital at Richmond where for the next four years she would record its social and political life.

Her journal is also a record of one woman's inner turmoil over marriage and family, her childlessness, her mixed feelings about slavery, hardship, and shortage, and the constant dread of defeat and ruin. By war's end she had written nearly half a million words. In the post-bellum years she intended to edit it down in size and see it published, but never finished the task, leaving it to others when she died November 22, 1886. It finally saw print in 1905 as *A Diary from Dixie*, and instantly became one of the most important and influential sources for Confederate and Southern history. A vastly better and more complete edition appeared in 1981 as *Mary Chesnut's Civil War*, and saw her endless hours over her journal recognized by winning the Pulitzer Prize.

JOHN LINCOLN CLEM

Even children went to war, sometimes without their parents' consent, but more often as "mascots" of regiments commanded by their fathers, or as musicians, especially drummers and fifers. Of course they were not supposed to go into battle, but now and then the circumstances turned these boys into men with unexpected speed.

John Clem was born in Newark, Ohio, August 13, 1851, and was only nine years old when the war broke out. He ran away from home actually hoping that he could enlist, only to be refused because he was barely half the age then required. Refused enlistment into an Ohio regiment, he attached himself to the 22d Michigan Infantry and simply followed the outfit, lurking on its periphery, until the colonel allowed him to act as a drummer. Of course he was not regularly enlisted, but the officers adopted him and paid him a soldier's wage to do camp chores.

Young Clem, now ten, was with the regiment as a drummer when it fought at Shiloh on April 6-7, 1862, and a Confederate cannon ball destroyed his drum. Almost overnight the Union press, anxious for heroes and inspiring stories, took the story of the little boy and his drum and made him "Johnny Shiloh." A celebrity in his own right, Clem continued to serve with his regiment, and was finally regularly enlisted in the regiment as a drummer, with full pay and allowances. At Chickamauga in September 1863 he carried a specially made small musket and rode atop a cannon carriage into battle. During the Union rout, when a Confederate ran after the carriage hoping to capture it or him, young Clem used his musket to shoot the soldier down. Once more the headlines lionized him, this time calling him "the drummer boy of Chickamauga." Following Chickamauga, Clem was in action around Chattanooga, at Lookout Mountain, and then in 1864 served with his regiment in the march across Georgia, fighting at Kenesaw Mountain, in the action around Atlanta, and the final battle of the campaign at Jonesboro. While the rest of the army marched on to the sea with Sherman, Clem and his outfit stayed behind, at one point serving as headquarters escort for their army commander General George H. Thomas, the "Rock of Chickamauga," before finally mustering out at the close of the war.

In all Johnny Clem would be wounded in action twice during the war, and for his bravery and his service President Grant in 1871 gave him a commission as lieutenant. Clem would serve in the United States Army for the next 45 years, rising to the rank of major general. He died May 13, 1937, the only drummer boy of the war to rise to such heights.

THE CONFEDERATE SOLDIER OF 1861

Nearly a million men would enlist in the Confederate armed forces during the course of the war. A fourth of them would never come home again. They covered every scale on the social ladder from aristocratic planter to illiterate farm laborer. The one thing they had in common when the crisis came was their youthful enthusiasm, a sense of regional patriotism, and a bright and optimistic outlook for the future.

As soon as Florida seceded on January 10, 1861, local volunteers and state militia quickly seized forts commanding Pensacola harbor and captured the navy yard at nearby Warrington. They failed to take Fort Pickens, however, sitting as it did isolated out on Santa Rose Island. Instead, volunteers from Mississippi and Louisiana and Alabama flocked to Pensacola to build a small army to lay siege to the fort. They came even before there was a Confederate government formed to command or coordinate their efforts, and they came in every description of clothing, and carrying weapons that had nothing in common with each other except their lack of uniformity.

In the photograph these Mississippi volunteers are garrisoning Fort Barrancas, and posing beside one of the mortars aimed at Fort Pickens. They display an awkward formality as they pose for the camera of pioneer cameraman Jay D. Edwards, who came from New Orleans with his camera to be the first true photographer of the war. Indeed, most of these men had never been in front of a camera before, nor for that matter had they ever served in the military.

While in and around Pensacola, photographer Edwards made upwards of sixty images. Sadly many no longer survive, but in the score or more that do, we have the most complete extant record of the look of the first Confederates, at work, at play, and in poses such as this, playing at what would soon become a deadly business indeed.

There is only one apparently complete uniform to be seen. Instead, some wear hats of an old Mexican War pattern, a few are in homespun shirts approximating uniforms, several wear leather cross belts, most have bandannas around their necks, and many have state militia belt plates at their waists. As for the rest, they wear whatever they had on when they left home. The officer presumably in command wears trousers with a stripe sewn on and a simple civilian frock coat, with military shoulder straps sewn on to indicate his rank as he stands on the mortar carriage. Yet it was out of such raw material as this that the Confederacy produced one of the finest fighting men in history. They never became real soldiers—just civilians on loan to the military—but they made history at the price of their blood and their lives.

GEORGE AND THOMAS CRITTENDEN

It was often called the "Brothers' War," and with good reason. Yet there were some families that took sibling rivalry just a bit far, virtually pitting brother against brother. If one such family could symbolize the conflicting loyalties that tugged at all of them, it had to be the Crittendens of Kentucky.

John J. Crittenden spent half a century in state and national politics. When secession came after the election of Lincoln, Crittenden introduced resolutions in the Senate designed to give North and South time to cool passions short of disunion and war. The Crittenden Compromise failed, and Crittenden thereafter went home to try to keep Kentucky from seceding.

But now the national tragedy repeated itself in his own family. His oldest son George Bibb Crittenden, born March 20, 1812, graduated from West Point in1832, and made a career of the military. He served in the Black Hawk War, then in the army of the Republic of Texas, then in the war with Mexico. By 1861 he had risen to the rank of lieutenant colonel but resigned his commission and "went South." A lifetime of friendships among the predominantly Southern officers of the army no doubt swayed his loyalty, as well as his own sympathy, as a Kentuckian, for fellow slave states. Jefferson Davis immediately made him a brigadier general.

His younger brother Thomas Leonidas Crittenden, born May 15, 1819, made the law his career, though in the war with Mexico he served as colonel of the 3d Kentucky Volunteers. Afterward he held a diplomatic post in England, then continued his practice at home until the war came. His loyalty bound him to the Union. He got a commission as brigadier general in September 1861.

Only misfortune prevented the two brothers from facing each other in action. George, soon promoted major general, lost the only battle in which he ever commanded, at Mill Springs, Kentucky, in January 1862. Accused of drunkenness at the battle, he was briefly arrested and almost court martialed, but soon commanded the reserve corps of the army marching to battle at Shiloh. Just days before the fight he was found drunk and relieved of command, and resigned his commission in October 1862. His brother Thomas was at Shiloh, and soon rose to major general and command of the XXI Corps, but the collapse of his command at Chickamauga in September 1863 ruined him. He, too, resigned, in December 1864.

Happily the brothers were reunited after the war, George serving as state librarian before his death in 1880, and Thomas as state treasurer before he returned to the army, dying in 1893. They are buried together in Frankfort, Kentucky.

ALONZO CUSHING

In a war in which tens of thousands performed heroically, still there were a few whose behavior in action so ennobled them that they became storied for all time. Some of them became virtual martyrs.

Alonzo H. Cushing (seen far left in the photograph) came from a family of young men whom some said were all a bit crazy. His brother William became a daring and notorious naval commander for the Union, leading landing parties on night missions behind Confederate lines, and commanding the dramatic raid that destroyed the Rebel ironclad Albemarle. Alonzo himself, born in 1841 in Waukesha City, Wisconsin, secured an appointment to West Point and graduated 12th in his class of 1861, just in time for the outbreak of the war. Immediately the War Department assigned him as a first lieutenant in the 4th United States Artillery, commanding a battery that he led at Bull Run.

Thereafter he performed well in virtually all of the battles of the Army of the Potomac, and developed such a loyalty to his battery that he passed up opportunities to transfer that would have brought promotion as well. He also showed a coolness and bravery under fire that won him two brevet promotions, at Fredericksburg and Chancellorsville.

Then came Gettysburg. Young Cushing was serving temporarily on the staff of General Winfield Scott Hancock when they arrived late on July 1, 1863, but returned to his battery that evening. Cushing was not heavily engaged the next day until early evening when he helped repulse the assault on Cemetery Ridge. On July 3 he sat out the bombardment that preceded the great assault of Longstreet's corps, then saw the wave of Confederates advance. Cushing's battery was only a few yards from the point towards which the advance aimed, and soon he was in the thickest of the fight. As the Confederates briefly broke through the Union line, Cushing feverishly sent volley after volley into the gray ranks. All of his officers fell, three of his guns were disabled, and Cushing himself took a painful wound in the right shoulder, and then another in the groin. Still he fought for half an hour or more, and in the final repulse of the enemy was beside his last working cannon, and had just fired a final shot as a Confederate bullet hit him in the head, killing him instantly.

He had helped turn the tide of battle for Union victory. When he died he was just 22, his battery destroyed with him. For his valor he would receive a posthumous promotion and burial among the heroes at West Point beneath a simple stone that says: "Faithful until Death."

GEORGE ARMSTRONG CUSTER

A fellow officer once described him as a "circus rider" gone absolutely mad. With his black velvet sailor shirt, long reddish ringlets, and red bandanna, it was obvious to one and all that George Armstrong Custer liked attention.

"Autie," as he was called from youth, was born near Scio, Ohio, December 5, 1839, and dreamed from youth of being a soldier. He grew up with his sister's family, and taught school briefly in the mid-1850s, but West Point was always on his mind. Legend had it that he finally got an appointment to the Military Academy thanks to the influential father of a local girl because he did not appreciate Custer's attentions to his daughter. He entered the academy in 1857 and achieved one of the worst records—short of dismissal—in its history, finishing last in his class in June 1861. Nevertheless, with the war just starting, he was immediately commissioned and sent to the army advancing into Virginia, where he saw his first action at Manassas in July. Somehow Custer got a staff appointment with General George B. McClellan, commanding the Army of the Potomac, and later on with the staff of General Alfred Pleasonton, commander of the army's cavalry.

He was undeniably bold and daring,, and for two years showed himself a fearless and useful officer. In the cavalry fight at Aldie, Virginia, on June 17, 1863, he led a portion of Pleasonton's cavalry under orders from the general, and so distinguished himself that on June 29, 1863, with little warning, he was elevated several ranks to brigadier general and given a brigade. Two days later he led it at Gettysburg, in the cavalry fighting east of the main battlefield, and led it well.

Custer participated in all of the cavalry fighting of the army subsequent to Gettysburg until he was transferred to the Shenandoah in the fall of 1864. There he led a division in battle at Winchester and Cedar Creek, then returned to the Army of the Potomac for the final campaign to Appomattox. Custer's division was instrumental in blocking the path of Lee's retreat, and compelling the surrender.

Though he finished the war a major general, Custer reverted to lieutenant colonel of the new 7th United States Cavalry, and with it his destiny would be linked until he and more than 200 of his men were killed on the Little Big Horn on July 25, 1876. Though his spectacular death always overshadowed his Civil War service, he had been, for all his faults and vainglory, one of the finest of the "boy generals" of the war.

THOMAS CUSTER

The Civil War was not just a case of brother against brother, but far more one of brother with brother. Whole families went to war and, as with the Cushings, many of them achieved distinction. None became more famous than the Custers of Michigan.

The career of George Armstrong Custer long ago entered the realm of American legend. "The Boy General," they called him, and indeed at one time he was the youngest major general in American history. As his performance as a Union cavalryman made him headlines and won him promotion, he brought one of his brothers up the rungs of notoriety with him. Born March 15,1845, Thomas was five years younger than George Armstrong and he and his own younger brother, Boston Custer, worshipped George. What he did, they did. In 1861 when George graduated from West Point and went to war, Thomas, though only 16, enlisted in the 21st Ohio Infantry.

Young Thomas Custer had a routine war until late 1864. By then brother George was a dynamic major general of cavalry serving in Virginia's Shenandoah Valley, and he succeeded in appointing Tom to his staff as a lieutenant. The brothers were devoted to each other, and remained together through the end of the war. The two shared many things, not least their temperament and reckless daring. During the Appomattox campaign, as Grant pursued Lee to the final surrender, the Custers participated in all of the actions that dogged Lee. On April 3, 1865, at Namozine Creek, Tom Custer rode straight over the defenses of the 2nd North Carolina Cavalry and personally captured their flag and captured several soldiers as well. The feat won him the Medal of Honor. Then, just three days later, at Sayler's Creek, Tom did it again, this time riding over defenses and personally killing a Rebel color-bearer as he grabbed the banner from the soldier. That soon won him a second Medal of Honor, making him the only soldier twice decorated with the nation's highest honor in its history.

Tom Custer continued to follow his older brother after the war, serving along the Rio Grande for a time. Younger brother Boston joined them when he became old enough. They were all together in the 7th United States Cavalry on June 25, 1876, and they died together at the Little Big Horn, Tom and George meeting their ends almost side-by-side. But while George was sent to West Point for burial, Tom was buried in the national cemetery at Fort Leavenworth, and Boston was sent home to Monroe, Michigan. They had paid the highest price possible for daring and heroism.

JOHN ADOLPH DAHLGREN

For all of the great reputations made by generals North and South, relatively few men in the naval services achieved fame, chiefly because it was predominantly, first to last, a land war, and those seamen who did gain notoriety usually did so with operations in tandem with the armies. One such was John Adolph Bernard Dahlgren.

He was a Pennsylvanian by birth, born in Philadelphia November 13, 1809, the son of the Swedish consular agent. All he ever wanted was to be a sailor. Denied an appointment as a midshipman when he first applied, he enlisted in the Navy in 1826 and gained years of experience before finally getting a commission. Soon he did duty with the United States Coast Survey and then in 1847 was assigned to the Ordnance Department at the Washington Navy Yard. He soon acquired considerable note for his experimental designs for naval cannon, and some of his inventions, especially the Dahlgren Gun—often called the "soda pop bottle gun" because of its shape—a heavy iron deck cannon that would be the workhorse naval gun of the Civil War.

Dahlgren was still in Washington when the war began, and in 1862 was named chief of the Bureau of Ordnance. However, he wanted a shipboard command, and fortunately had cultivated good relations with President Lincoln. Consequently, in February 1863 Lincoln appointed him a rear admiral and gave him command of the South Atlantic Blockading Squadron. Dahlgren was not a popular man, conceited, willful, unabashedly self-serving. Moreover, he was somewhat boastful, and on taking command let it be known that he expected to capture Charleston in a hurry, and preferred to do it without the army's help.

In fact, however, he would never set foot in Charleston until after the army captured it in February 1865. Instead, he cruised off the South Carolina and Georgia coast, and nearly lost his life late in the war when his flagship Harvest Moon struck a Confederate underwater mine and sank in five minutes. His son was not so fortunate. Colonel Ulric Dahlgren, just 21 years old, led a cavalry raid on Richmond in February and March 1864 with the intent of getting into the city and capturing or killing Jefferson Davis. It all went wrong, and young Dahlgren himself was killed, a loss from which his father never entirely recovered. Admiral Dahlgren himself stayed in service after the war, seeing duty in the Pacific, and then returning to his real sphere of achievement, the Ordnance Bureau. Now in command of the Washington Navy Yard, he died there July 12, 1870.

JEFFERSON DAVIS

He had a middle name that he never used. It was Finis, Latin for "the end," and for Jefferson Davis, most of his endings were unhappy ones.

Davis was born June 3, 1808, in Kentucky, and grew up in southern Mississippi, near Woodville. He went to Transylvania University in Lexington, Kentucky, for two years, but then accepted an appointment to West Point. Graduating 23d in his class in 1828, he spent the next seven years in the army. In 1835 he left to set up as a planter at Brierfield, a plantation near Vicksburg, and married the daughter of General Zachary Taylor, but she died three months later of malaria and he nearly died of it as well.

Davis spent the next decade largely in seclusion, but in 1845 married Varina Howell of Natchez, and won a race for Congress as a Democrat. The war with Mexico called him to the colonelcy of the 1st Mississippi Rifles, and at Buena Vista he became a bona fide hero. After the war Davis served Mississippi briefly as a senator, and then spent four years as secretary of war for President Franklin Pierce. When secession came, Davis was in the Senate again. While he always believed in the right of secession, he hoped for compromise almost until the end, then resigned his seat and returned to Mississippi to become major general of state troops.

Almost immediately, however, the Provisional Congress in Montgomery elected Davis president. When he arrived to take his oath of office, a leading secessionist said, "The man and the hour have met."

Davis's presidency was controversial from the first, as he tried to lead a nation composed of unionists, arch-secessionists, and several tiers of opinion in between. He built the army almost single-handedly, and always retained too tight a grip on appointments and promotions. He surrounded himself with sycophants, tried to attend to too many details himself, alienated much of Congress, and never established a rapport with the Confederate people. Nevertheless, no one's heart was more in the cause. He sustained generals like Lee, took considerable risks, and probably kept the Confederacy afloat longer than any other man would have. In the end, he was almost the last to admit defeat. Captured and imprisoned for nearly two years, he hoped for a trial that would vindicate himself and the South, but the United States decided not to try him.

For the rest of his life Davis struggled. He outlived all but one of his six children, lost most of his property, and was bedeviled by acrimonious attacks by Beauregard, Joseph E. Johnston, and others, battling it out with them in his own memoirs, *Rise and Fall of the Confederate Government*. When he died in New Orleans December 9, 1889, he was, if not loved, at least revered.

JEFFERSON C. DAVIS

One would hardly think that a Union general would be so unfortunate as to have the same name as the Confederate president, but such was the case, and that was not the only misfortune to befall this Indiana farmboy.

Jefferson Columbus Davis was born March 2, 1828, and when not much out of school volunteered for the 3d Indiana regiment that was going to the war in Mexico in 1846. He fought with it at Buena Vista, and after the war decided to stay in uniform, taking a commission as a lieutenant in the 1st United States Artillery. Thirteen years later he was still a lieutenant in the artillery, only stationed at Fort Sumter in Charleston Harbor, and was with his command when the Confederate guns opened fire on the fort and the Civil War commenced. Like many other Regular Army officers, he opted for much higher rank in the volunteer service and took the colonelcy of the 22d Indiana when they were raised.

Davis performed well, and a few months later commanded an Indiana brigade at Wilson's Creek in Missouri, for which performance he won a brigadier's star and command of a division. He led it at Pea Ridge in March 1862, and then brought it east of the Mississippi to aid in the siege of Corinth that summer. Furloughed on sick leave to Cincinnati, and though still unwell, he helped organize the defense of Louisville during the Confederate invasion of Kentucky, and commanded a battalion under General William "Bull" Nelson. Prickly natures on both sides led to Nelson slapping Davis's face in the bar of the Galt House in Louisville, and a few minutes later Davis returned with a pistol and shot Nelson fatally.

Briefly incarcerated, Davis was never brought to trial in the murky affair, and soon resumed active duty, though he would never receive another promotion, though richly deserved. He fought ably at Stones River and Chickamauga and in the Atlanta Campaign, rising to command of the XIV corps by the fall of 1864. Sherman himself attested to Davis's ability as a combat commander, but despite stellar service in the March to the Sea and the final campaign in the Carolinas, the second star of a major general was not to be his. After the war Davis reverted to Regular Army rank of colonel of the 23d United States Infantry, and served in the brief Modoc War in California, as well as in Alaska for a time. He died prematurely on November 30, 1879, in Chicago.

VARINA HOWELL DAVIS

There may not necessarily be a good woman behind every successful man, but if ever a man needed such a woman, it was the president of the Confederate States of America.

Jefferson Davis married twice. His first wife—surely the real love of his life—was young Sarah Know Taylor, daughter of President Zachary Taylor. But she died after only a few months of marriage when both contracted yellow fever. Davis himself nearly succumbed, and thereafter spent almost a decade in mourning and seclusion. Then in 1845 his brother Joseph arranged for him to meet Varina Howell. She was born in Natchez May 7, 1826, and was eighteen years his junior. She did not like Davis at first, but some mutual attraction brought them together and they soon married.

Temperamental differences, exacerbated by Davis's absence in Congress and then in the Mexican War, made their early years unsettled, and twice Davis left her briefly until she learned to curb her natural outspokenness and independence. Thereafter she made an ideal political wife, especially for the austere, aloof, and sometimes offensive Davis. Outgoing, intelligent, well educated, she fitted perfectly into the social scene in Mississippi and in Washington, and readily made the transition to First Lady when Jefferson was chosen president of the Confederacy.

Varina's personality proved to be a valuable asset, especially in smoothing the feelings that her often graceless husband ruffled. Indeed, some in the South rumored that she was a power behind the throne, and certainly it was true that those who offended her often saw their Confederate careers flounder. She was also the object of jealousy and backbiting from those who opposed her husband, some even hinting that her dark complexion meant she was a mulatto. Yet none could fault her work for relief of the poor and the wounded. The only reason that Jefferson Davis was captured on May 10, 1865, while fleeing from the Yankees, was that he refused to separate himself from his wife.

After the war, she worked relentlessly to get Jefferson freed from prison, and after his release she devoted herself to him and raising their children—five of whom she would outlive—in the face of near impoverishment. She helped Jefferson with his memoirs, and after his death wrote her own, which reveal that she still had an independent mind after all, and which provide the best insight we have into her husband's seemingly unfathomable personality. She died, universally revered in the South, on October 16, 1905, a thoroughly modern woman who was in many ways well ahead of her time.

MARTIN DELANEY

"I want to tell you one thing," a speaker said to a black audience shortly after the close of the conflict. "Do you know that if it was not for the black men this war never would have been brought to a close with success to the Union, and the liberty of your race if it had not been for the Negro? I want you to understand that."

The speaker was Martin Delaney, and even if his claim was somewhat exaggerated, the fact remains that nearly one tenth of the Union army was made up of free Northern blacks and escaped Southern slaves. Even if they were not the decisive factor that he claimed, certainly the war would not have been won as it was without them.

Delaney was one of them. His origins are obscure, but he was already connected with the great black orator and freedom fighter Frederick Douglass before the war started. In the 1850s, despairing of his people achieving full equality, he favored for a time the policy of recolonizing blacks back to Africa, but then in 1861 he, like Douglass, saw in the war an opportunity to advance their race closer to equality by pressuring the Washington government to allow them full participation in the conflict. If the nation allowed them to fight and die like white men, it could hardly afterward deny them the right to live like whites.

Almost immediately after the War Department authorized raising black regiments, Delaney joined Douglass and other prominent abolitionists in speaking to rallies throughout the Northeast to raise volunteers for the first outfit, the famed 54th Massachusetts. Inevitably, Delaney himself eventually enlisted, and demonstrated in action the same ability he had shown as a recruiter. Eventually he would be one of a handful of blacks to be awarded the Medal of Honor for valor, but Delaney would outstrip his fellows in another way. Even though more than a hundred regiments of black troops were raised, the Negroes themselves were restricted to the enlisted and non-commissioned ranks. Their officers were exclusively white, and there was considerable opposition both in Washington and in the field armies' high command to giving blacks commissions as officers.

Ultimately, however, about 100 blacks won commissions in spite of the opposition, all of them as lieutenants except for one captain. Martin R. Delaney, however, sufficiently won the confidence of his superiors that on February 26, 1865, he was promoted major of the 104th United States Colored Troops, a regiment he helped to raise. He was the highest ranking black of the war, though his promotion came at a time when the conflict was virtually over and he never led his regiment in the field. After the surrender he continued to hold his commission until 1868 as sub-assistant commissioner of the Freedmen's Bureau, under assignment to help oversee the transition of former slaves to freedom.

FREDERICK DOUGLASS

The Civil War era was one made for the emergence of dynamic leaders to fit the crisis. Not all of them were generals and politicians, and not all of them were white. Fittingly, in a conflict that came about more than anything else because of the debate over slavery in American society, one of the most dynamic leaders of all was a former slave.

He was born sometime around 1817 near Tuckahoe, Maryland, named Frederick Augustus Washington Bailey, the son of a slave woman and an unknown or unacknowledged white father. He grew to manhood as a slave, but showed a rebellious nature from an early age, and ran away more than once, only to be caught and returned to face sometimes a severe beating. By the time he was 21, however, he had grown large and powerful, and finally defied his owner, telling him that he would never be beaten again, and he never was. In 1838 he ran away for the last time and made good his escape to the North, at the same time changing his surname to Douglass.

Frederick Douglass arrived in Massachusetts in 1841 as the ferment over abolition was rapidly heating up, and someone hearing him speak, and impressed both by his booming voice and his obvious raw intellect, arranged for him to address the convention of the Massachusetts Anti-Slavery Society. That began his career as the most forceful and eloquent exponent of abolition. The Society employed him as one of its agents, and soon thereafter he began writing his first book, *Narrative of the Life of Frederick Douglass*, which appeared in 1845, and told the world, in the words of a literate slave, of the evils of slavery.

Thereafter Douglass was in the forefront of the abolition movement. He lectured widely, chiefly retelling his own experiences as a slave, and once having to flee abroad to escape slave catchers still hunting him. In Europe he earned enough from his lectures that he was able to return and purchase his freedom, and not long afterward raised enough to publish an abolition newspaper the North Star, named for the celestial guide that runaway slaves followed in escaping northward.

When the Civil War came, Douglass began steady pressure on the Lincoln administration to allow black regiments to join in the fight, and after they were enlisted he continued the struggle to get them equal pay and allowances. His own son served in the Union army, and in the end he could take pride in seeing more than 170,000 free blacks serve under arms. After the war he continued struggling for justice and equality, including equal rights for women. The government rewarded him for his career with several political appointments, including that of minister to Haiti and United States marshal for the District of Columbia, where he lived until he died in 1895.

J. L. DOWLING

When the Civil War broke out, there were at least 3,000 men—and a few women—professionally practicing the art of photography. They used a myriad of techniques and processes—ambrotypes, melainotypes, daguerreotypes, calotypes, cartes-de-visite, stereo views, and more. A few hundred of them went to war to follow the armies, most famous of all being Mathew Brady and the dozen or more artists that he sent into the field. Even the United States Army had one official photographer. For a few of these cameramen, however, the war and the armies came to them.

New Bern, North Carolina, was a peaceful backwater of the war until Federal troops occupied the Atlantic seaboard community in 1862-1863. Awaiting them there was local photographer J. L. Dowling. There were no battles in New Bern, no action to capture on camera, but for several months Dowling took his camera out to record the camps and installations of the Yankee occupiers, and hundreds of them came to his second floor studio above a drug store to have their portraits taken. In all, more than a million photographs were taken during the war, over 99 percent of them soldier portraits, which were the bread and butter of photographers, there being little profitable market for outdoor scenes.

On the cool day when this photograph was taken, probably in the fall of 1862, men of the 25th Massachusetts Infantry came to Dowling's studio, where officers and enlisted men posed outside for the cameraman. But there was another sitter in this pose, showing the imagination and enterprise—as well as the penchant for self-promotion—that characterized so many of the artists of the war. For Dowling had at least two cameras. One he set up outside the studio to capture the men in their varied poses. The other he set up in the second floor window of his studio, and placed himself behind it, thus photographing himself at work.

Of Dowling himself we know nothing more than that he practiced his craft in New Bern, and all he left behind to remember him by is the body of his work that has survived, showing a quiet, almost idyllic, forgotten spot of the war. The photographers were nearly as fascinated with themselves as with the war and, like Dowling, many stopped amid capturing the scenes of the conflict, to record themselves recording it, leaving us a dramatic portrait of the infant industry of photo-journalism aborning.

PERCIVAL AND THOMAS DRAYTON

The war split families and brothers in every conceivable variety of ways, but none more bizarrely than two men from South Carolina who were destined to face each other in battle on the very soil where they played as boys.

The Draytons were an old family in the Palmetto State. Thomas Drayton (inset) was born August 24, 1808, in Charleston, and his younger brother Percival appeared almost fours years later to the day, on August 25, 1812. They grew up together in the Low Country, and both chose the armed services as careers. Thomas entered West Point in 1824, becoming a close friend of cadet Jefferson Davis, with whom he graduated in 1828. Thomas Drayton remained in the army only for eight years, however, then returned to South Carolina to become a planter and a state politician. Brother Percival, meanwhile, secured an appointment as a midshipman in the Navy in 1827, and thereafter remained in uniform, slowly gaining in rank to be a commander on the eve of the Civil War.

The secession of South Carolina tested the loyalties of both. Thomas chose to stand by the state of his birth, and his friendship with the new President Davis easily gained him a commission as brigadier general in September 1861. His was not destined to be a happy war. He never escaped the odium of getting his commission thanks to favoritism, and his poor performance did not help. After service in South Carolina, he was attached to Longstreet's Corps of the Army of Northern Virginia, and led a brigade at Second Manassas and Antietam so badly that Lee took the brigade away from him, and Drayton spent the balance of the war banished to minor commands west of the Mississippi.

Percival, by contrast, did well for himself. Having spent most of his adult life at sea and in Philadelphia, he sided with the Union. In October 1861 he commanded the USS *Pocahontas*, then in the summer of 1862 rose to captain commanding a warship in the South Atlantic Blockading Squadron, when he aided in the 1863 naval attack on Charleston. He eventually rose to fleet captain under David G. Farragut, commanding the *Hartford* in the Battle of Mobile Bay.

The defining moment for them came on November 7, 1861. The Union fleet attacked Port Royal, South Carolina, with Percival Drayton's *Pocahontas* in the vanguard of the bombardment of Confederate Fort Walker. The fort was commanded by General Thomas Drayton. Knowing this, his brother took the *Pocahontas* closer to the fort than any other warship, for fear that his superiors would think he quailed from attacking his own brother. The Federals won, but the brothers were never reunited. Percival died on August 4, 1865, with the war barely over, while Thomas lived until February 18, 1891.

DAVID GLASGOW FARRAGUT

On a dramatic day in August 1864, one of the Union's mightiest machines of war, the ironclad monitor USS Tecumseh suddenly lurched in the water of Mobile Bay, Alabama, and sank within seconds, taking all but one man aboard to the bottom. She had struck an underwater mine, then called a torpedo. Looking on from his perch in the shrouds of the flagship USS Hartford, a native Southerner who had become the Union's greatest naval commander refused to allow the danger of other mines to avert him in his attack on the Confederate fleet awaiting him. "Damn the torpedoes!" he said.

The United States was just twenty-five years and a day old when James Glasgow Farragut was born July 5, 1801, not far from Knoxville, Tennessee. It was a long way to the sea in any direction, but his ferry operator father soon moved to New Orleans for a navy position, and there the Farraguts became closely involved with the family of the famed David Porter, one of the young nation's first naval heroes. After his father's retirement, Farragut became the ward of Porter's son, and with his help won an appointment as a midshipman in 1810. Four years later, Farragut changed his first name from James to David in appreciation.

He would spend the rest of his professional life in the uniform of the United States Navy, winning one plaudit after another. He commanded his first prize ship in the War of 1812 at the age of only 12 years. After the war he served in the Mediterranean, then the West Indies, slowly rising in rank until he settled in Norfolk, Virginia, in 1823, where he married and remained until the outbreak of the Civil War.

In 1861, now a captain, Farragut left Virginia when it seceded and hoped for a significant command, but it was not until January 1862 that he took over the West Gulf Blockading Squadron. He built up the fleet that captured New Orleans in April 1862, and thereafter cooperated in the attack on Vicksburg, meanwhile closing all Confederate ports on the Gulf except Mobile. While his foster brother David Dixon Porter helped Grant take Vicksburg in July 1863, Farragut assisted in the bombardment that led to the surrender of Port Hudson a few days later.

His last great objective was Mobile, heavily defended by forts and Confederate warships. On August 5, 1864, he steamed past the forts, ignored the torpedoes, and captured or dispersed the enemy fleet, with the forts soon surrendering. Lincoln promoted him to vice admiral, the first ever, and two years later Congress created the rank of full admiral for him. The war ruined his health, however, and he died September 30, 1870, still on active duty.

NATHAN BEDFORD FORREST

Some thought he was the devil himself. He personally killed more enemy soldiers than any other general of the war, and knifed one of his own officers to death in a brawl. There was nothing halfway about the man who liked to "get there first with the most."

Nathan Bedford Forrest was born July 13, 1821, and grew up in semi-poverty. When he was 24 he killed a man who shot his uncle in a fight, then a few years later moved to Memphis. He engaged in the cotton trade, but increasingly found selling slaves profitable, and became a man of some wealth. When Tennessee seceded in June 1861, he enlisted as a private in the mounted rifles, but a few weeks later raised his own cavalry battalion and became its lieutenant colonel.

He showed a natural aptitude for the mounted service, with spectacular results. In February 1862 he helped open the escape route for besieged Confederates at Fort Donelson, Tennessee, and when timorous commanders pulled back, he refused to do so and led his men to safety. He fought at Shiloh, and that summer, after capturing a Yankee garrison at Murfreesborough, he became a brigadier and accompanied Bragg's army on the invasion of Kentucky. Afterward he recruited a new brigade in Tennessee with which he became a terror to Union commanders in west Tennessee.

He did not get along with superiors, however, almost fought with two generals, and after the Battle of Chickamauga he threatened to whip Bragg. Nevertheless Forrest rose to major general and continued his raiding, including the controversial fight at Fort Pillow, near Memphis, on April 12, 1864, where several score white and black Federal troops were killed after they tried to surrender, and Forrest apparently lost control of his men. Thereafter he was the bane of Federals in the region, then in the fall accompanied the Army of Tennessee on the ill-fated campaign to Nashville.

The government made this untutored genius of war a lieutenant general in March 1865, but by then even Forrest's prowess could not affect the outcome. Surrendered May 4, he tried to rebuild his fortunes, but failed at planting, the insurance business, and railroading, and died October 29, 1877, with even his memory somewhat tarnished by his two years as Grand Wizard of the Ku Klux Klan. Time has never diminished his greatness as a cavalryman, however. The assertion—probably mythical—that some of the great armor commanders of World War II studied and emulated his campaigns, is testimony to the regard in which he is held today as a chieftain.

ULYSSES S. GRANT

He was a man who failed at almost everything, but when he found the one thing he could do well, he did it perhaps better than anyone else of his time.

He was born Hiram Ulysses Grant at Point Pleasant, Ohio, on April 27, 1822. Through friends his father secured him an appointment to West Point, but an error led to his name being mistaken as Ulysses Simpson Grant, a change that he found it simpler to adopt than to correct. Grant excelled only in horsemanship, despite which he was placed in the infantry. In the war with Mexico, he served in Zachary Taylor's army in the 4th United States Infantry, and then under Winfield Scott, and saw action that won him plaudits and promotion.

The peacetime that followed found Grant at a Pacific coast outpost, depressed and lonely, and finding solace in drink. He resigned in 1854 and then tried a succession of trades, and failed at all of them. Then came the war, and he offered his services to the governor of Illinois. In June he was commissioned colonel of the 21st Illinois regiment, then in August he was made a brigadier. He commanded at Cairo, Illinois, and then occupied Paducah, Kentucky, in September. His first battle came in November with a brisk skirmish at Belmont, Missouri.

In February 1862 he moved his growing command to capture Forts Henry and Donelson, opening up most of Tennessee to the Union and forcing the enemy to evacuate western Kentucky. Despite a surprise at Shiloh in April, he turned it into a victory, and thereafter focused his attention on the capture of Vicksburg and control of the Mississippi. Stymied time after time, he kept on coming, until finally on July 4, 1863, Vicksburg was his. By now he was a major general and the Union's most successful commander, and he continued his progress that fall when he lifted the siege of Chattanooga, then routed Braxton Bragg's army at Missionary Ridge.

Lincoln responded by making Grant a lieutenant general, the first since Winfield Scott, in March 1864. With it came overall command of all Union armies, and thereafter Grant planned the coordinated offensives across the continent. He placed himself with the Army of the Potomac, and largely directed it against Lee at the Wilderness, Spotsylvania, and Cold Harbor, then executed a brilliant crossing of the James River without Lee's knowing it, and narrowly missed taking Richmond and Petersburg. When that failed, he besieged Lee for ten months, and finally surrounded him at Appomattox.

A full four star general at the war's end, Grant went on to become embroiled in Reconstruction politics, then won two terms as president. He left office in 1877, and spent his last years struggling, at one point bankrupt, and fighting a race with cancer to finish his memoirs. He won by a matter of days, and when he died July 23, 1885, he left behind one of the finest military autobiographies of all time.

JENNIE HODGERS

It should hardly be a surprise that not just the young men of America felt their blood pulse when war erupted. Women felt the same patriotism, the same excitement, and not a few wanted somehow to share in the experience. A few actually did in every respect.

In 1861, as for millennia previously, women's role in war was assumed to be almost nonexistent. The Civil War would change that, seeing thousands serve as nurses, and drawing tens of thousands more into the work force for the first time to replace men gone to the armies. A few girls even became "vivandiers," regimental mascots of a sort, with uniforms and marching like cheerleaders when regiments went on parade, though when the men went to the front the vivandiers usually stayed home. For some, however, that was not enough. No one knows the exact count, but perhaps as many as 300 or 400 young women actually posed as young men and enlisted to fight.

One was Jennie Hodgers of Belvidere, Illinois. She was actually Irish by birth, born Christmas day 1844, but left home and came to America as a stowaway before the war, revealing already a nature bent on adventure. On August 6, 1862, the slightly built girl, not yet 18, dressed as a man and enlisted as a private in the 95th Illinois Infantry. Fortunately for her, enlistment physical examinations were less than perfunctory, and for the rest of the war no one saw through her disguise. She became Albert Cashier, and served with her unit through the Vicksburg campaign in the summer of 1863, then went to Louisiana for the Red River campaign the next year, then into Mississippi, fighting Nathan Bedford Forrest at Brice's Cross Roads, seeing action in Missouri that fall, and then in the inferno at Nashville in December 1864. She served right to the end, mustering out in August 1865 as a sergeant.

Her messmates knew Cashier as a quiet fellow who kept to himself. That and her straight, slim build helped Hodgers keep her secret. Indeed, she kept up the impersonation for the next 46 years, until she was struck by an automobile in 1911 and a doctor discovered her gender. Crippled and unable to care for herself, Hodgers actually gained entry to the Quincy, Illinois, Soldiers and Sailors Home for two years until she lost her sanity and was moved to an asylum. On October 11, 1915, she finally died, her secret only then becoming generally known. She had received her full soldier's pension for years, and her old comrades of the 95th Illinois buried her in her uniform. There are two headstones on her grave at Saunemin, Illinois. One is a civilian marker with the name Jennie Hodgers. The other is a regulation United States Army veteran's stone placed by the government, and bearing the name of Albert Cashier.

THE IRON BRIGADE

It was inevitable that some units would become more storied than others, more famous for their valor or their sacrifice. Fighting qualities helped, but so did other intangibles, even uniforms. One such became known as the "Black Hat Brigade" thanks to their headgear, but there was another sobriquet ahead of them when, after the summer of 1862, they became known to posterity simply as the Iron Brigade.

The brigade began in the Old Northwest, where in the first months of the war Wisconsin enlisted and sent to the front three regiments, the 2nd, 6th, and 7th Infantries. Before long they formed a brigade with the addition of the 19th Indiana Infantry, and then after the Battle of Antietam, and the frightful depletion of the brigade's numbers, authorities added the 24th Michigan Infantry. They were issued a pre-war army pattern hat called the "Jeff Davis" thanks to the fact that it had been adopted when now-Confederate President Jefferson Davis had been secretary of war for President Franklin Pierce. The stiff, high crowned hat, with one side of the brim clasped up, was widely used in the western Union armies, but these men were the only ones to wear it in the Army of the Potomac, and thus the headgear always seemed to be identified with this brigade, hence its first nickname.

Then came South Mountain. After already being blooded at Second Bull Run, the unit showed exemplary courage under fire in the Battle of South Mountain, holding their ground against superior numbers of the foe, and leading General George B. McClellan to comment that they stood like iron. Thus was born the Iron Brigade, and these stern soldiers would wear their black hats and their new name with grim pride in the coming inferno at Fredericksburg, and Gettysburg to follow.

The great battle in Pennsylvania cost the brigade 65 percent casualties, and in the 24th Michigan losses ran to 80 percent, almost all of them incurred on the first day of fighting as they struggled to delay a Confederate juggernaut long enough for the balance of their army to arrive on the field. Gettysburg all but destroyed the brigade. Its name would go on until the end of the war, but the brigade itself was never the same, the staggering losses replaced by the addition of new regiments and even draftees. But before it disappeared in the maelstrom of July 1-3, 1863, it achieved an unrivalled name among the storied units of Civil War history.

Thomas Jonathan Jackson

Only Robert E. Lee himself has attracted more reverence than his most famous lieutenant, the man called "Stonewall." So great is his hold on the American imagination, that he is the only Confederate general who, some believe, had his life been spared, might have changed the outcome of the war.

He came from the humblest beginnings. Born January 21, 1824, in Clarksburg, Virginia, he was left an orphan by his father's early death, and was raised by a cold and unloving uncle. Secured an appointment to West Point in 1842, he struggled at his studies, mastering by rigorous rote. When he graduated in 1846, he ranked a respectable 17th in his class, and almost immediately went off to war in Mexico, where he performed well in battle. The years after the war proved disappointing, however, and in 1851 he resigned to take a position as a professor at the Virginia Military Institute at Lexington.

Lexington would be his home for the rest of his life. A devout Presbyterian, and an uninspired teacher, he succeeded by determination, just as at West Point. His students ridiculed him, and one allegedly tried to kill him, yet most left the VMI with a grudging respect for the man they called "Tom Fool." Jackson was no secessionist, nor was he passionately attached to slavery, but when Virginia seceded in April 1861 he followed his state into the Confederacy.

What followed is the stuff of legend. After a brief period drilling recruits in Richmond, he was commissioned a brigadier and assigned command of the 1st Virginia Brigade. He led them at the First Battle of Manassas, or Bull Run, and there they both earned an immortal sobriquet when another Confederate general likened their stand in battle to that of a stone wall.

Promotion came quickly and, as Major General Jackson, Stonewall led his command back to the Shenandoah where in the spring of 1862 his combination of lightning movement and deft strategy defeated three separate Union forces greater than his own. He fought with Lee in the Seven Days Battles, and then in August won a considerable victory at Cedar Mountain on his own. At Second Manassas he set up Lee's victory, then fought at Antietam and Fredericksburg, by now a lieutenant general commanding the II Corps of Lee's army.

His greatest day, and his last, came on May 2, 1863, at Chancellorsville, where he led his corps in a wide flanking march around the Union right, and struck a stunning surprise blow that put a whole Federal corps to rout. But accidental shots from his own men left him seriously wounded. Eight days later he died of complications. When he was buried in Lexington, much of the hope of the Confederacy was buried with him.

ALBERT SIDNEY JOHNSTON

Late in 1861 Jefferson Davis lay in his room at the Confederate executive mansion, ill, gloomy, and worried. Then he heard someone enter the front door. "That is Sidney Johnston's step," he said at the familiar sound.

Davis and Johnston met at West Point. Born in Kentucky February 2, 1803, Johnston went to Transylvania University and then entered the military academy in 1822, two years ahead of Davis. He finished in 1826, eighth in his class, and went on to a varied and distinguished career. He served in the Black Hawk War, then in 1837 resigned and moved south to become a general, and secretary of war of the Republic of Texas. In the war with Mexico he served on Zachary Taylor's staff, then in 1849 reentered the United States Army and served on the frontier until commissioned colonel of the elite 2d Cavalry. By 1861 he was a brevet brigadier general commanding the Department of the Pacific.

When Texas seceded, Johnston resigned and made the long trek to Davis's front door to offer his services. He found a commission as the senior ranking field officer of the Confederate Army awaiting him, such was Davis's confidence. Johnston went west to command Department No. 2, embracing everything between the Mississippi and the Appalachians, an impossible command, tens of thousands of square miles with far too few troops. Feverishly, Johnston began building an army, while trying to hold every inch of ground possible.

His first disappointment came at Forts Henry and Donelson in February 1862, when Grant used gunboats on the Tennessee and Cumberland Rivers to support his army. Fort Henry fell almost without a defense, and Donelson was surrounded and forced to surrender. As a result, Johnston abandoned Kentucky and all of middle and west Tennessee, but he rebuilt his army in northern Mississippi, determined to push Grant back. He planned a splendid concentration of forces from as far away as Florida, and led a forward march so well covered that on the eve of the Battle of Shiloh Grant did not believe that Johnston's army was anywhere near him.

On April 6 Johnston launched one of the greatest surprise attacks of the war, and at first he had all his own way, as the Yankees steadily fell back before him. That afternoon a bullet struck him behind the knee and he either ignored it or did not feel the wound, as he bled into his boot. With victory seemingly in his grasp, he fell from his saddle and never spoke a word, dying minutes later. Davis ever after mourned his loss, thinking Johnston would have risen to heights as a commander even greater than Lee's. He remains one of the great "what ifs" of the Civil War.

JOSEPH E. JOHNSTON

Ironically, both of the Confederate Johnstons were "what ifs," Albert Sidney because he died before he could show his capability, and Joseph E. Johnston because—he maintained—he never got a fair chance.

This Johnston was a Virginian, born February 3, 1807, the son of a distinguished Revolutionary War soldier. In 1825 he started at the Military Academy at West Point, and finished four years later 13th in his class. He spent the next 32 years, excluding a few months, in the United States Army. In the Seminole War and the war in Mexico he served well, winning repeated promotion, so that by 1860 he was quartermaster general of the army, with the temporary staff rank of brigadier general, though his actual field rank remained that of lieutenant colonel.

When Virginia seceded, Johnston took command of the state militia, and then shortly afterward President Davis made him a brigadier general in command of marshaling forces in and around Harpers Ferry. Johnston defended the Shenandoah Valley that spring, then moved his small army east to join forces with Beauregard to defeat the Federals at First Manassas on July 21. He remained in command of the combined armies and was skipped over the grades of major and lieutenant general, to the grade of full rank general, just behind Samuel Cooper, Albert Sidney Johnston, and Robert E. Lee in seniority. That began a controversy that poisoned his relations with President Davis, for Johnston felt that he should outrank the others.

In 1862 Johnston faced the Yankees on the Virginia Peninsula, falling back steadily before them until the Battle of Seven Pines, where he took a dangerous wound. He did not return to duty until November, when Davis assigned him to overall command west of the Appalachians. Johnston did not like the command, and did little with it, fighting Davis more than he did the enemy. His dilatory action helped doom Vicksburg and its garrison, but still in December 1863 Davis assigned him to command the Army of Tennessee after Bragg's resignation. Johnston led the army in the Atlanta Campaign, repeatedly falling back before the enemy until an exasperated Davis relieved him on July 17, 1864, only adding to the acrimony between them. In February 1865 Johnston commanded the army again, but it was a skeleton by then, and his only contribution was to help force Davis to accept that the war was lost. Johnston surrendered his own army without authorization on April 26, virtually ending the war east of the Mississippi.

Afterwards Johnston fought Davis with a vigor he never showed against the Yankees. Joining with other dissident generals like Beauregard, he waged the battle of the memoirs with his own *Narrative of Military Operations* in 1874, and at last had the satisfaction of outliving Davis, dying March 21, 1891, a man whose battlefield promise—if it was ever there—he never fulfilled.

PHILIP KEARNY

Some officers were especially beloved by their men and fellow leaders, none more so than Philip Kearny, one of the finest soldiers of the pre-war army, and one whose promise was tragically unrealized in the Civil War.

He came from New York city from a family of wealth and position, and was the nephew of the explorer and Mexican War hero General Stephen W. Kearny. Young Kearny, born June 2, 1815, himself wanted a military career, but instead his family sent him to Columbia University where he graduated in 1833. Thereafter he studied law but before he could enter into practice an unexpected inheritance of $1 million freed him of the necessity to pursue that profession, and bought him the luxury of turning to his first love. Thanks to family connections he secured a commission as a lieutenant in the 1st United States Dragoons in 1837, where he quickly attracted attention as perhaps the finest horseman in the army. In 1839 the army sent him to France to study cavalry tactics, and while there he saw his first action with a French unit at Algiers.

In the war with Mexico he did escort duty with General Winfield Scott, and lost his left arm after a severe wound in battle at Churubusco. After recovery he remained in the military until 1851, when he made a world tour with his new wife, retired briefly, then went to France to act on Napoleon III's imperial guard in his campaign against the Italians. Kearny repeatedly demonstrated his gallantry in cavalry charges, riding with his reins in his teeth.

At the outbreak of the Civil War, he returned to the United States and quickly received a commission as brigadier general on August 7, 1861. He led a brigade of New Jersey regiments in the Peninsular Campaign in the spring of 1862, then rose to major general and a division command. He led his division well in the Yankee defeat at Second Manassas in August 1862, and then went into action in the minor engagement at Chantilly on September 1. The Confederates aimed their rifles at him and yelled out to him to surrender. It was a common enough occurrence in this war. Half a dozen generals were either killed or captured when they inadvertently rode beyond their own lines. To a man of Kearny's dash, capture was unthinkable, however. On horseback as usual, he accidentally rode beyond his own lines and suddenly found himself in front of a Confederate position. He wheeled his horse and made a dash for safety, but a Rebel volley cut him down. Kearny was as mourned in the Confederate army as in his own, and Robert E. Lee himself sent his old friend's body back across the lines. Winfield Scott had called him "the bravest man I ever knew, and a perfect soldier."

RICHARD KIRKLAND

Out of wars come many nicknames, all too many of them redolent of the inhumanity of men—"beast," "butcher," and worse. But out of the inferno of Fredericksburg came one man to be known for all time as an "angel."

Richard R. Kirkland was born near Flat Rock, South Carolina, in August 1843 and raised by his father. After secession he and his brothers enlisted, Richard mustering into the Confederates' Company G of the 2nd South Carolina Infantry. He was with his regiment at Charleston when Fort Sumter was fired on, and a few months later he saw his first action in the Battle of Bull Run.

His moment came at Fredericksburg on December 13, 1862. It had been a day from hell. Confederate infantry strongly placed on Marye's Heights repulsed one hopeless attack after another as Union forces absorbed more than 12,000 casualties. In the bitter winter cold a man could have walked across the field stepping on the bodies of the wounded and slain. For hours the Confederates heard the cries of the wounded, pleading for water in their pain. Kirkland finally went to his brigade commander Brigadier General Joseph Kershaw.

"All night and all day I have heard those poor people crying for water, and I can't stand it any longer," he said. "I came to ask permission to go and give them water." Kershaw gave him permission, but would not let him go out between the lines with a white handkerchief for safety, since it might be taken as a surrender. Before long the men of two armies saw the young soldier crawl over the wall carrying canteens. Amid the pulsing volleys, stepping from one downed Yankee to another, he gave them water, covered one with his own overcoat, and kept at his mission of mercy for more than an hour. Both sides soon held their fire, and from the Union lines came cheers of thanks and admiration.

His act made Kirkland a celebrity briefly assigned to recruiting duty, but he rejoined his command in time to win a commission at Gettysburg. But then came Chickamauga. In the waning action on Snodgrass Hill, a Federal bullet struck him in the chest. He lived only long enough to tell comrades, "I am done for. You can do me no good. Save yourselves and tell my Pa I died right."

More importantly, he had lived right. Ironically, his own brigade history scarcely mentions him, and attributes his heroic act to an unnamed Georgian. But Richard Kirkland is well remembered elsewhere, with monuments at Chickamauga and Fredericksburg, and a simple plaque at Gettysburg recalling that "at the risk of his own life, he gave his enemy drink." To posterity he will never be forgotten as "the Angel of Marye's Heights."

ROBERT E. LEE

If ever a man was born to be a hero, it was Robert E. Lee. Born January 19, 1807, in Westmoreland County, Virginia, he was the son of a hero, "Light Horse Harry" Lee of the Revolution, and a descendant of one of the "First Families" of the old Dominion. Being a Virginian would dominate his life.

He entered the United States Military Academy in 1825, and graduated second in his class in 1829, to spend the next 36 years in uniform. Lee saw wide and varied service, but it was in combat that he excelled. In the war with Mexico he served on the staff of General Winfield Scott, performing dangerous scouting missions that were integral to American successes. Peacetime found Lee in quieter roles, including superintendent at West Point, though in October 1859 he commanded the contingent that fought and captured John Brown's raiders at Harpers Ferry. In 1861 Lee had the opportunity for high command with the Union, but with Virginia's secession he followed her fortunes. Briefly he commanded the state militia until President Davis commissioned him a brigadier, and later a full rank general. But Lee's Civil War did not start well. He failed in a command in western Virginia, then commanded the defenses of South Carolina, and by early 1862 was stuck as military advisor to the president in Richmond.

When Joseph E. Johnston fell wounded at Seven Pines in May, Lee got his chance. Davis gave him the command of what would become the Army of Northern Virginia, and the general and the army were never apart for the rest of the war or posterity. In a dazzling campaign Lee drove the Federals away from Richmond, then struck north, defeating them on the old Manassas battlefield before launching his first invasion of the North, ending at Antietam. Despite that setback, Lee inflicted a severe defeat at Fredericksburg in December, and the next May, at Chancellorsville, won the most crushing battlefield victory of the war. Elated with his success, he gambled on another invasion, but was stopped at Gettysburg in July.

The spring of 1864 pitted Lee against a new antagonist, U. S. Grant, and only Lee's tactical brilliance prevented Union numbers from pushing him aside. At the Wilderness and Spotsylvania, the North and South Anna, and Cold Harbor, Lee repeatedly stymied Grant, who nevertheless kept coming. By June Lee had his back to Richmond, and no alternative but to accept being besieged. For the next ten months he held Grant at bay, but in early April all the options were gone. Lee and his army made a dash to the west, but Grant caught them at Appomattox, and there on April 9, 1865, Lee surrendered.

Lee spent his last years trying to rebuild his Virginia and discourage sectional enmity. He took the presidency of the failing Washington College at Lexington, and built it into a fine institution, later to be Washington and Lee University. He died in Lexington October 12, 1870, and mourned the North and the South as a symbol of dignity and conciliation.

ABRAHAM LINCOLN

His enemies called him tyrant and dictator. His own generals called him ugly and a gorilla. But his troops and the people at home called him "Father Abraham," and, like the patriarch of old, he led a people to freedom.

Abraham Lincoln's life seems one of those happy accidents in which nothing turned out as would have been expected. He was born into frontier poverty on February 12, 1809, the son of a semi-literate farmer in Hodgenville, Kentucky. His mother died when he was still a child, and he received no more than a few months of formal schooling, but he was bright and largely taught himself. He grew into a strapping six foot, four inch young man, with a greater preference for books than for the plow and axe.

Once he reached his majority and could leave his father's house, Lincoln moved to New Salem, Illinois, and there started life as a laborer and store keeper. He saw brief volunteer service in the Black Hawk War in 1832, and was ever after proud of his brief military service. Meanwhile he studied the law and hung out his shingle in 1836, and in 1834 he won his first race for a seat in the legislature. He served eight years all told, and moved to the capital in Springfield, where in 1842 he married Mary Todd of Kentucky. Lincoln opposed the Mexican conflict when it commenced in 1846, and spoke against it when he won his one term in Congress in 1847. A Whig in politics, he increasingly identified himself with anti-slavery factions, and when the Whigs dissolved after the war, Lincoln joined the new Republican Party which was dedicated to stopping the further spread of slavery.

In 1858 Lincoln ran for the Senate against Stephen A. Douglas, and though he lost, their series of debates made him a national figure, and defined the political crisis facing America. Consequently, in 1860 he became the Republican nominee for the presidency, and won the election when the Democrats split and ran two candidates. Lincoln was pledged to keep the Union together, and never recognized the right of secession, yet hoped to avoid conflict. The firing on Fort Sumter changed that, and thereafter his overriding policy was to end the revolt and bring the Southern states back into the Union.

Few expected this shambling, ungainly westerner to be an effective president, but in fact he proved to be a brilliant manager and executive, consistently rated the greatest of American presidents. He had the patience to deal with defeat and keep trying, the humanity to share his people's sacrifices, and the eloquence to give voice to their pain and aspirations. After one bad general after another he found Grant, and after four years he forged the victory and was poised to manage a gentle peace, when an assassin's bullet cut him down on April 14, 1865. "Now he belongs to the ages," one of his cabinet supposedly said at his deathbed. Indeed he does.

RANALD S. MACKENZIE

In a war with many "boy generals," this one stood out, as he would after the war when he daringly led his command across an international border at considerable risk to himself and his nation.

Mackenzie was not even young Ranald Slidell's last name. He was born in New York July 27, 1840, in the prominent Slidell family, his uncle being John Slidell, Louisiana planter and future diplomat for the Confederacy. His father added the Mackenzie name, and it was as Ranald Mackenzie that the young man entered West Point in 1858 after three years at Williams College. Ironically, while he was at the Military Academy, his uncle by marriage, P. G. T. Beauregard, was superintendent. The youth did well, finishing first in his class in June 1862, to find a commission and a war waiting for him.

Mackenzie served first as an engineer, but soon moved to the combat arm, and saw battle at Second Manassas, Antietam, Fredericksburg, Chancellorsville, Gettysburg, and the Wilderness, before finally getting a colonelcy and command of the 2d Connecticut Heavy Artillery in June 1864. He commanded his unit—really just an outsized infantry regiment—in defending Washington against a Confederate raid that summer, then took an assignment in the Shenandoah where General Philip H. Sheridan was trying to clear the Valley of Confederates. It was under Sheridan that Mackenzie, like Custer and other young men, really blossomed. He soon commanded a brigade before being wounded at Cedar Creek in October, then transferred to the Army of the Potomac after recovery, and received his commission as brigadier. Now under Grant's eye, Mackenzie led a division of cavalry, and Grant himself remarked that, "I regarded Mackenzie as the most promising young officer in the army."

After the war Mackenzie reverted to colonel, and led the 4th Cavalry in operations against the Indians on the central plains and in the southwest. In 1873 he actually took his regiment across the Mexican border to run down Apache marauders, risking an international incident. Then he took on the Cheyenne in the wake of Custer's Little Big Horn debacle, and forced their surrender. In all, his service covered almost the whole of the West until he retired in 1885 as a brigadier general, still aged only 44. Repeatedly wounded during the Civil War and after, his health was shattered and he lived in retirement less than four years before his death January 19, 1889, his mind disordered from the pain he had suffered.

Lincoln said he had "the slows"; others thought he simply lacked the moral courage to endanger his reputation by taking risks. Everyone expected him to be a great soldier.

George Brinton McClellan was born to affluence in Philadelphia, December 3, 1826, and received his appointment to West Point in 1842. Four years later he finished second in his class just on the outbreak of the war with Mexico. McClellan performed ably as an engineer during the advance from Vera Cruz to Mexico City, and best of all won Winfield Scott's admiration. Subsequently he taught at West Point, went overseas to observe the Crimean War, and participated in surveys for the future transcontinental railroad. He even designed a cavalry saddle that bore his name and remained in use well into the twentieth century.

McClellan left the army in 1857 to work for the Illinois Central Railroad, but as soon as war broke out many in high places remembered the promising officer. The governor of Ohio commissioned him a major general of state militia in April 1861, and a few weeks later President Lincoln made him a major general in the Regular Army, with only Scott himself outranking the man now called "Little Mac." After a successful minor campaign in Western Virginia, he was called to Washington to assume command of the beaten army from First Manassas.

"Little Mac" had an unusual gift for infusing elan into the men. He trained and equipped them into the Army of the Potomac, one of the finest ever seen on the continent. But when it came to leading them in the field, he proved hesitant and reluctant, always needing more men, forever convinced that the enemy outnumbered him. Appointed general-in-chief on November 1, 1861, he did not move until spring to advance on Richmond by way of the peninsula southeast of the city, but he was badly beaten by Lee in the Seven Days battles. He blamed Washington for his failure, attempted to dictate civil policy to Lincoln, and failed to support General John Pope in northern Virginia, leading to another defeat at Second Manassas.

McClellan somewhat redeemed himself when he stopped Lee's invasion of Maryland at Antietam, but virtually let Lee get away when he had been trapped. Thereafter he delayed and complained again, until Lincoln relieved him of command on November 7. He was still awaiting orders for two years, when the Democrats nominated him to oppose Lincoln's reelection in 1864. Soundly defeated, he resigned his commission, served as governor of New Jersey, and devoted his last years to his bitter, mendacious, vain memoirs. He died October 29, 1885, never having lived up to his other nickname, "the young Napoleon."

JAMES B. MCPHERSON

Only two army commanders would be killed in action during the Civil War, one on each side. Albert Sidney Johnston was one, mortally wounded at Shiloh on April 6, 1862. The other was a popular young man from Ohio who rode off into the woods near Atlanta and never came back.

James Birdseye McPherson was born November 14, 1828, with none of the advantages enjoyed by many of his future classmates at West Point. He came from the lowest ranks of the poor, and only the help of others got him an appointment to the Military Academy. Once there, however, he excelled on his own, and finished in 1853 first in his class. During the next eight years as an engineer, he attracted wide notice for his ability and promise, and when the Civil War broke out General Henry Halleck attached him to his staff in Missouri. Soon afterward McPherson transferred to engineer duty on Grant's staff, and the friendship between them blossomed, McPherson's subsequent rise accompanying that of Grant's.

McPherson was with Grant through Forts Henry and Donelson, Shiloh, and on through the Iuka Campaign, meanwhile rising to colonel in May 1862, and brigadier general in August, and occasionally seeing more action than usual for staff officers. No doubt with Grant's heavy backing, he rose yet again to major general on October 8, 1862, and was given command of a division. In January he assumed command of the XVII Corps and led it capably during the Vicksburg Campaign, winning special honors at Champion Hill. Late that winter he served under Sherman in the Meridian Campaign, and in March 1864 assumed command of the Army of the Tennessee when Sherman rose to army group commander.

When Sherman commenced the Atlanta Campaign, McPherson was his most trusted army commander, and Sherman used him time and time again for the long flanking marches that steadily forced the Confederates back into the Atlanta defenses. Finally on July 22 McPherson set out to do this again, this time facing Confederates in the city's earthworks, and while riding out on a personal reconnaissance, he was apparently caught in the path of an unexpected enemy counterattack. His men saw his riderless horse come galloping back into their lines, and later found his body in the field. Sherman was said to have wept at the news, and even the imperturbable Grant was deeply affected by the loss of a good friend and one of the most universally loved officers in the Union army.

FRANCIS R. NICHOLLS

In the Louisiana campaign for governor in 1876, the Democrats nominated and elected what they called "all that is left of General Nicholls." It may have been humorous, but it was hardly a joke.

Born in Donaldsonville, Louisiana, on the Mississippi River on August 20, 1834, Francis Redding Tillou Nicholls had family political connections which secured him an appointment to West Point in 1851, and he graduated four years later in the top fourth of his class. He served only two years before illness forced him to resign, then studied law in New Orleans and commenced practice just as secession came.

Nicholls raised a small company of volunteers, then soon raised another and served as its captain before being elected lieutenant colonel of the 8th Louisiana. He went with the regiment to Virginia and fought at First Manassas, then served under Stonewall Jackson in the Shenandoah Valley. At the Battle of Winchester on May 25, 1862, a bullet destroyed his left elbow and the arm had to be amputated. At the same time he was captured by the Federals and he spent three months as a prisoner before being exchanged.

On his release Nicholls was promoted colonel of the 15th Louisiana and sent to Texas, but a month later he received his commission as brigadier general and assignment to command the Louisiana brigade with the Army of Northern Virginia. His first battle with the army was Chancellorsville, and there on May 2 a cannon ball killed his horse and ripped off his left foot. Given up for dead at first, he was finally treated and left to ponder his fate—two battles fought, and two limbs lost. By the summer of 1864 he was recovered enough to assume post command at Lynchburg, Virginia, then transferred west of the Mississippi where he finished out the war raising troops.

Nicholls went back to the law at the end of the war, and like so many others in Louisiana faced trying to resuscitate a state economically ravaged by the war by turning to politics during the Reconstruction years. When he was elected governor in 1876 a question over the balloting led to both he and his opponent running simultaneous administrations for a time before Nicholls' election prevailed. Nicholls himself joked that he might have preferred being a judge, but with his left arm and foot gone he was "too one-sided" for the bench. When he left the governor's mansion, he tried the law for a time, and served as president of the board of visitors of the Military Academy at West Point, before winning another term as governor. He then spent almost twenty years on the state supreme court, dying January 4, 1912; honored in the South and respected in the North.

OFFICERS OF FORT SUMTER

With the war not even begun, some photographers sensed the importance of what was coming, and got themselves ready to record for all time the holocaust about to sweep America. Not only did the Southern states make the conflict almost inevitable when they tried to leave the Union, but the very first true photographers of the war were themselves Confederates.

The first prisoners of war were captured not by enemy troops, but by the camera of Charleston photographer George S. Cook. A few days after South Carolina seceded, the garrison at Fort Moultrie on Sullivan's Island found itself exposed and in imminent danger, and by stealth in the night evacuated to the much stronger Fort Sumter in the middle of Charleston Harbor. There the garrison, under the eyes of gathering Confederate volunteers, would be a continuing thorn in Southern pride until finally, on April 12, 1861, the surrounding batteries opened fire and forced the surrender of the outgunned and outnumbered Federals.

Weeks before, however, Cook took his camera out to Fort Sumter on a February afternoon and persuaded the commander and his officers to sit for their portraits. In this image the assistant surgeon, Captain Samuel W. Crawford, stands at the back. He would rise to major general in the war ahead and lead first a brigade and then a division with distinction in action at Gettysburg and elsewhere. And after the war he wrote one of the best histories of the opening action of the war at Fort Sumter. Seated on the right is Captain Truman Seymour, and he, too, would rise to a general's stars, fight at Antietam, and then come back to participate in the siege of Charleston in 1863. By war's end he commanded a division in the army that forced Lee to surrender at Appomattox. Seated on the left is Lieutenant Theodore Talbot, who might well have become a general, too, except that he fell early in the war ahead, victim of the greatest killer of all, disease.

Cook made other images, one of Anderson by himself, and another of all the fort's officers, including a lieutenant named Jefferson Davis who would become a Union general, and Lieutenant R.K. Meade of Virginia, who fought loyally in defending the fort on April 12-13, 1861, and then resigned his commission to enlist with the Confederacy. Little did any of them know as they posed for Cook that day in February what lay ahead for them and their torn country. Even as Cook advertised his images in Charleston with the tongue-in-cheek claim that he had "captured" the garrison's officers, these men were just weeks away from being the first true prisoners of war, even if only for a few hours before their release. They were the first of hundreds of thousands.

OLD ABE

Incredibly enough, even the animals of America were caught up in the spirit of the conflict. Regimental mascots by the hundreds went into the camps with the soldiers, the overwhelming majority of them beloved dogs that all too often went down in battle. But there was one Yankee mascot that quite literally rose above the battle for the only true "bird's eye" view of the conflict enjoyed by any participant.

When Company C of the 8th Wisconsin Infantry was recruiting in 1861, Mrs Daniel McCann offered something special to the regiment. A few months before she had encountered some Flambeau Indians on the banks of the Chippewa River, and in trading with them she found they had a young eagle chick recently taken from the nest. Taking it home with her, she made a pet of the bird, taming it sufficiently that it would keep to its perch without needing to be tethered. Now she offered the eagle as a mascot to the new company of recruits, and they gladly accepted. In honor of the new president, the eagle was named "Old Abe."

He was an instant hit with the army. The soldiers built a special perch for him backed by a Union shield, and on parade the bird seemed to catch the spirit of the affair and spread his wings and shriek for the crowds. Soon the 8th Wisconsin became known as the "Eagle Regiment," and Confederates recognized them in action too, thanks to "Old Abe." Their first action was at New Madrid, Missouri, in March 1862, and thereafter the eagle participated in some 42 actions, including Island No. 10, Corinth and Iuka, Vicksburg, the Red River Campaign, and the initial phases of the fall campaign in Missouri. "Old Abe" seemed stimulated by battle. At the first shots he left his perch and flew over the battlefield, often flying over the Confederates and screeching at them while they tried unsuccessfully to hit "the Yankee buzzard" as they called him, then with the battle done he returned to his perch.

Late in September 1864 the regiment gave him to the state, and he spent his remaining years in a special cage in the state capitol at Madison, but often came out for veterans' parades and special events. More photographs of him were sold for family albums than of any soldier or other animal of the war. He lived on, venerated, until smoke from a fire in the Capitol killed him. He was stuffed and mounted and put on display, only to be lost in another fire, but "old Abe," whom they called "the war eagle," lives on as statues of him preside over the Wisconsin state assembly.

ELY S. PARKER

"I am glad to see one real American here," General Robert E. Lee said in the McLean house at Appomattox on April 9, 1865. He had come to surrender his army, and hardly expected to find among the Yankee officers awaiting him a full-blooded Seneca sachem.

Ely S. Parker was born the son of a Seneca chief in 1828 at Genesee, New York. The Seneca by then were increasingly—though not fully—incorporated into white culture in New York, and as a result he went to both white schools and Seneca. He studied law at first, but discovered that not being white he could not take the bar to practice in New York, and thus he turned to engineering at the Rensselaer Institute, graduating in 1857. One of his first jobs took him to Galena, Illinois, where he became acquainted with U. S. Grant, then working as a merchant in the city, and the two became friends.

At the outbreak of war Parker tried to enlist, but was denied because of his race, and it took almost two years before he secured a commission as captain and adjutant on the staff of General John E. Smith in the Army of the Tennessee. Grant helped him get the position, and soon thereafter he transferred to Grant's staff as his military secretary. As Grant rose, so did Parker, and on August 30, 1864, he was promoted to lieutenant colonel. When Appomattox came, and after Lee's complimentary greeting, Parker transcribed Grant's notes to produce the actual surrender documents, and reminded Lee that "we are all Americans now."

Parker remained with Grant until 1867 when he resigned his commission—which included a brevet promotion to brigadier general to date from the day of the surrender—until Grant took office as president, when he appointed Parker commissioner of Indian affairs, the first native American ever to hold the post. His tenure was not a happy one, however, in part due to prejudice. He was investigated by Congress, harassed by well meaning but inept do-gooders, and expected to favor unscrupulous contractors.

Discouraged, he later resigned and went into business, at which he failed. He made a fortune on the stock market in later years, but then mirrored his friend Grant's financial misfortunes when he lost it all. His last years were dogged by sorrow, made all the more painful from having risen so far in what was a white man's world. Despite his poverty, however, he would always be revered by his people for having achieved so much, and deserves to be remembered for his declaration to Lee that "we are all Americans." By the time of his death August 31, 1895, he was impoverished, his only remaining possession of any value one of the copies he had made of the Appomattox surrender paper.

JOHN PELHAM

"It is glorious to see such courage in one so young." It was at the Battle of Fredericksburg in December 1862 that General Robert E. Lee said those words as he watched the heroic performance of a twenty-four year old artilleryman. In a young man's war, some stood out for coolness and daring under fire, but none more so than the youth that Lee and others called "the Gallant Pelham."

John Pelham was born in Benton, Alabama, September 14, 1838, and went to West Point just short of his eighteenth birthday. There he fell under the influence of Major Henry J. Hunt, who would later be chief of artillery of the Union Army of the Potomac. Pelham showed an affinity for the artillery, and would have graduated high in his class but for the outbreak of the war. Though Alabama seceded in January, 1861, Pelham remained at West Point until April 22, after actual hostilities had broken out, before he left shortly before graduation.

Pelham accepted a commission as lieutenant in the artillery, and was on the field at the First Battle of Bull Run in July, where his performance first attracted the attention of his superiors. Made a captain, he was given command of the horse artillery attached to General Jeb Stuart's cavalry, and remained with Stuart for the rest of his short life. Pelham's forte was the rapid movement and deployment of his guns, keeping pace with cavalry actions, and using mobility to make up for the frequent disadvantage in firepower. At Antietam, now a captain in recognition of his services at Second Bull Run and elsewhere, he deceived the Federals into thinking his battery was in fact a much larger force, then surpassed that performance at Fredericksburg where Lee gazed so approvingly upon him. On the right of the Confederate line, with only two cannon available, he kept up such a rate of fire and kept moving them from point to point so quickly, that he delayed the advance of an entire Union division that thought it faced several batteries.

Pelham also accompanied Stuart on his famed raids, and quickly became associated with Stuart himself as romantic ideals, Pelham the more so since he was unmarried, handsome, and made the young belles swoon. Sadly, at Kelly's Ford, Virginia, on March 17, 1863, he was watching a minor cavalry skirmish and decided to ride along on a charge, only to be mortally wounded. He died later that day, and was mourned throughout the army and the South.

GALUSHA PENNYPACKER

In a war in which boys became men overnight, one Pennsylvanian with the unlikeliest of martial names became a general even before he was old enough to vote.

He was born near Valley Forge on June 1, 1844, and saddled for life with the name Galusha Pennypacker. He was still just 16 when the war broke out, but he came of a martial heritage, his father a veteran of Mexico and his grandfather of the Revolution, and so young Pennypacker volunteered for the 9th Pennsylvania Infantry, and his company elected him a sergeant. A few weeks later he recruited a new company of his own that became part of the 97th Pennsylvania and elected him its captain, and soon thereafter he was promoted to major, while still only 17.

Pennypacker saw his first real active duty in the forgotten theater of Florida and on the South Carolina coast, including the operations around Charleston in 1863, and the fighting for Battery Wagner. Transferred to Virginia, he and his regiment were with the Army of the James in the fighting at Drewry's Bluff and around Petersburg, and he rose to lieutenant colonel of his regiment in April 1864, and then colonel in command of a brigade in the XXIV Corps in August. In the several assaults in the Petersburg Campaign, Pennypacker was wounded four times, but still recovered to return to duty. He was well liked by his men for his cheerfulness and reliability, even though many of them were some years older than he.

In December and January 1865 Pennypacker went with the Army of the James in the amphibious assault on Fort Fisher, near Wilmington, North Carolina, and in the final successful attack he was dangerously wounded, making a total of eight times that he was hit during the war. He was hospitalized for the rest of the year, but on February 15, 1865, while still only 20, he was promoted brigadier general. In addition to his other honors, Pennypacker later would be awarded the Medal of Honor (today called the Congressional Medal of Honor), for his service at Fort Fisher, where his commander declared that Pennypacker was the greatest hero produced in the action, and that without him the Yankees might not have captured the fort, thus spelling the doom of Wilmington.

After the war young Pennypacker stayed in the army as colonel of the 34th Infantry and later the 16th Infantry, which he continued to lead until his retirement in 1883, when not yet 40. After leaving the army he returned to Philadelphia, where he died October 1, 1916, a lonely bachelor whose adult years never matched the tremendous excitement of his youth.

THE POWDER MONKEY

The naval service differed from the army in a number of ways, thanks mainly to long pre-war tradition. For one thing, blacks served in the Union navy long before they were accepted into the land forces. For another, while males young enough to be children did occasionally manage to get into the regiments of the army, mere boys were commonplace on the warships of the Union fleet. Recruiting posters called for "all able bodied men and boys," and the youngsters came, legally eligible for enlistment at the age of twelve.

Most of them, like this jaunty youngster standing in front of a powerful Parrott rifle on the main deck of the USS *New Hampshire*, served as powder monkeys. In action it was their assignment to carry the bags of powder from the ship's magazine to the gun crews on deck. The job required them to be small, so they did not get in the way on a crowded and very active deck, and their youth helped to ensure their being fast. They wore slippers or cloth booties so there was no danger of a nail in their shoes striking a spark in the magazine, and they carried the powder—sometimes weighing 30 pounds or more—in oak buckets to prevent any powder that spilled from the bag being dropped on the deck where it might ignite. The powder monkey handed the bag to the gun crew, emptied any loose powder into a barrel of water, and then ran back for another.

When not in action, youngsters like this boy acted as ward room stewards and officers' servants, helping the ships' cooks, and performing any other odd jobs that did not require a man's strength or training. Their rank was simply that of "boy," though many rose as they got older to become able seamen. Few lost their lives in action, for naval battles were infrequent in this war. Most of their service on the big ships was blockading duty and sometimes convoying transport fleets for amphibious invasions. But they were subject to all the other perils of accident and disease, while service on a ship of full grown men exposed them to influences that would have shocked their parents. At least they shared the generally better food and more healthful conditions that characterized naval life, and a few of them got to go far beyond the horizons of their boyhood homes, traveling the rivers and seacoast of the Confederacy, and a few sailing the oceans of the world.

How many of these youngsters lost their lives we do not know, since many were not carried on the muster and pay rolls, and many Union ships never saw hostile action. But we do know that the tragedy of war reached down to the very youngest. There were boys of barely the age of ten who fell in battle on the land, and 13 and 14 year olds who never came home again were tragically common.

WINFIELD SCOTT

His soldiers in one war called him "Old Fuss and Feathers," and he was the only soldier in American history to command troops in three wars.

Winfield Scott almost defined the United States Army by 1861. Born a Virginian on June 13, 1786, he attended the College of William and Mary and studied law, but then in 1808 secured an appointment in the army from President Jefferson. Four years later when the War of 1812 came, he quickly rose to brigadier general, and distinguished himself in battle at Lundy's Lane, finishing the war a major general. During the ensuing years of peace he retained high command, and in 1841 was made commanding general of the United States Army. When the war with Mexico broke out in 1846, Scott wielded overall command and conducted a brilliant campaign from his landing at Vera Cruz through the march on Mexico City itself. However, he also conducted a political battle behind the lines, for he and President Polk were enemies, and Scott's aspirations for the presidency conflicted with those of the other great general of the war, Zachary Taylor. It was while in Mexico that Scott nurtured favorites like Robert E. Lee and George B. McClellan who were destined for future renown.

After the war Scott was promoted to lieutenant general and finally got a presidential nomination from the Whigs in 1852 but was defeated by Franklin Pierce. Worse was in store for him when he engaged in a much publicized feud with Secretary of War Jefferson Davis that plummeted into puerile name-calling. Yet in 1861 when civil war came, Scott still held overall command, though he was 75, and his huge six foot, five inch frame was now obese. Still, his mind was alert. Southerners regarded him as a traitor, a Virginian siding with the North, but he spurned all suggestions that he join the Confederate cause.

Scott spotted promising officers for promotion to take field commands of the Union's armies, and more than anyone else enunciated the overall strategy of constricting the Confederacy by land and sea that eventually won the war. Sadly, he was unceremoniously pushed out of office by McClellan, and he resigned November 1, 1861. Some, perhaps Scott himself, thought he had been a failure in the Civil War, and he was widely and crudely caricatured then and later. Yet he had served as the very model for two generations of the younger generals who were now to fight that war, and he as much as anyone proved the value of the Military Academy at West Point in its uncertain infancy, ensuring that it would live to produce the Lees and the McClellans and hundreds more. He lived to see the war won, and died at West Point May 29, 1866, leaving behind one of the most remarkable careers of any American soldier.

RAPHAEL SEMMES

Only one man in the Confederacy served both as an admiral and a general, and simultaneously at that. Not surprisingly, he was an officer used to standing out from the crowd.

Born in Maryland, September 27, 1809, Raphael Semmes grew up in the District of Columbia and in 1826 took a commission as a midshipman in the United States Navy, where he would serve for more than three decades. After several years of duty at the Norfolk Navy Yard, Pensacola, and Mobile, he took command of the USS *Somers*, which sank during the war with Mexico, and thereafter saw service chiefly ashore until 1861 and the secession of Alabama, his adopted home. On February 15 he resigned his commission and accepted one as a commander in the fledgling Confederate Navy.

At first the new government sent him north to buy ships and supplies from dealers willing to profit from the Confederacy before actual fighting began. Soon afterward the Navy Department put him in charge of light houses, but Semmes pressed for active duty at sea, and especially in one of the contemplated commerce raiders that were to prey on Union merchant shipping. Semmes himself was instrumental in securing the first of these, the CSS *Sumter*, and accepted command in the fall of 1861. In his first six-month cruise in the *Sumter* Semmes captured 17 Yankee ships before he decommissioned his little vessel.

He had greater things in view. The Navy purchased in England the specially built "290," a cover name for what became the CSS *Alabama*, and Semmes took command of her in August. Thereafter he made his name and hers the terror of Northern shipping. In 22 months he overhauled and captured 55 prizes, including one small Union warship. For almost two years Semmes put a fright into Union merchant shipping, until June 1864 when the USS *Kearsarge* brought him to bay off Cherbourg, France, and there on June 19 the Union got its revenge by sending the *Alabama* to the bottom.

Semmes himself escaped and went to England, but returned early in 1865 to take command of the James River fleet outside Richmond. There was little for him to do, and he had to destroy his own ships to prevent their capture when Richmond was evacuated. Then, to cap an amazing career, President Davis commissioned him a brigadier general on April 6 and put him in command of a small brigade during the flight of the Confederate government. Finally he was surrendered with the Army of Tennessee three weeks later. After the war Semmes was imprisoned for a few months as a pirate, but never tried, and after release he worked at the law and education until his death in Mobile, August 30, 1877.

ROBERT GOULD SHAW

"Onward, Fifty-fourth," yelled a young colonel to his regiment. They were the last words he ever spoke, but his outfit went onward, not just that day in 1863, but on into posterity, to make him and themselves legendary.

Robert Gould Shaw came of a noble old Boston family, well known for their abolition views. He was born October 10, 1837, and given his family's social position it was natural that he should enter Harvard University, bound for the professions. But young Shaw had a streak of independence, and a zest for the military life. He left school before graduation and went to New York, while there joining the elite 7th New York National Guard. On the outbreak of war he quickly returned to his native state and, thanks to family connections with Governor John Andrew, he secured a commission as a lieutenant in the 2nd Massachusetts, one of the first regiments raised.

Shaw served with his regiment from then on through Antietam. In February 1863, when Andrew received authorization to raise the first black regiments, he offered Shaw the command of what would become the 54th Massachusetts. At first Shaw turned it down, but soon changed his mind, and quickly threw himself into the challenging task of recruiting and training the new regiment. Met with ridicule and prejudice from many fronts, Shaw persevered, and by May had the regiment to go to war.

The War Department assigned Shaw, now a colonel and engaged to be married, to the forces besieging Charleston. He and the 54th saw no action at first until June when they were attached to a raid on Darien, Georgia, that turned into a humiliating looting spree in spite of Shaw's efforts, and for which he bore no responsibility. Then came orders to spearhead an evening assault on Battery Wagner on Morris Island on July 18. At 7:45 p.m. Shaw, having landed his regiment on the island, gave the order to advance along the beach toward the sand and earthwork fort.

They advanced at a run, under Confederate fire all the way, and then stormed up the outer works and onto the parapet itself. Shaw was in front, shouting his encouragement to the men, when a bullet killed him instantly and he fell inside the fort. Scores of his soldiers followed him in death in the failed attack, and the next day the Confederates buried them all together in a common grave. After the war, given the opportunity to have his son disinterred and brought back to Boston, Shaw's father declined, preferring to leave his brave son with the men for whose freedom he had died.

WILLIAM TECUMSEH SHERMAN

He may never have said that "war is hell," but few men on either side understood the truth of the phrase so well as the man who "broke hell loose" in Georgia.

Friends called him "Cump." Sherman's father admired the great Shawnee leader Tecumseh, and so honored him by naming his son for him. Born February 8, 1820, at Lancaster, Ohio, young Sherman was orphaned at an early age, and raised by friends, including Senator Thomas Ewing, who got him an appointment to West Point in 1836. In 1840 Sherman finished sixth in his class, but missed the real action in the war with Mexico, being stuck in California where little happened. Slow promotion afterward impelled him to resign in 1853, first for banking in San Francisco, then the law, and finally the superintendency of the Louisiana State Seminary and Military Academy.

Sherman was in Louisiana when the state seceded, and had close friends in the South and a genuine fondness for the region. But his loyalty was to the Union. On May 14 he received appointment as colonel of the 13th United States Infantry, and by summer commanded a brigade in the army beaten at First Manassas. Unlike many, he predicted a long and bloody war. Having performed well in his first battle, he was promoted brigadier in August, and later sent to defend Kentucky. Unfortunately he suffered a minor nervous breakdown, aggravated by exaggerated fears of enemy attack, and the press branded him "crazy Sherman." He quickly recovered, however, and commanded a division under Grant at Shiloh.

Thereafter Sherman's fortunes were linked with Grant's, each a perfect complement to the other. Commissioned a major general in May, Sherman was Grant's right arm for the next year in the operations leading to the capture of Vicksburg. Sherman went with Grant to relieve the siege of Chattanooga in November 1863, conducted his own campaign to Meridian Mississippi that winter, and in the spring of 1864 assumed command of several armies in the western theater and planned and conducted the famous Atlanta Campaign. Thereafter he marched his armies across Georgia and South Carolina to Savannah, cutting the Confederacy in two, and finished the war in North Carolina where he accepted the surrender of the Army of Tennessee.

After the war Sherman succeeded Grant as general-in-chief and four star general, and retired in 1884, thereafter refusing repeated requests to seek the presidency. He wrote his memoirs, one of the finest of their kind, and died February 14, 1891, in New York, one of the most fabled of all American soldiers.

FRANZ SIGEL

"I fights mit Sigel," his soldiers liked to say, though often as not he was likely to abandon them, yet no one was more potent in raising tens of thousands of immigrant volunteers for the Union.

Franz Sigel came from Baden, Germany, where he was born November 18, 1824. He attended the military academy at Karlsruhe, and on graduation in 1843 served under Grand Duke Leopold until the outbreak of revolution amid the wars of unification that inflamed most of Europe in 1848. After lackluster performances on the battlefield, he became minister of war on the revolutionary side, but when his forces were defeated by Prussia, he escaped to Switzerland, and eventually came to America in 1852. At first he taught school in New York, then moved to St. Louis, where he lived amongst a substantial community of fellow German émigrés. He was prominent in German-American activities, and consequently when the war came in 1861, Union authorities naturally turned to men like him hoping they could influence their comrades to enlist. Indeed, Sigel proved very successful in arousing the union-loving, slavery-hating immigrants to enlist.

On August 7, 1861, Sigel received a brigadier's commission, and fought in the Battle of Wilson's Creek, Missouri, where he performed poorly, abandoning his command at one point and fleeing to Springfield. Yet he survived this and fought well the next March at Pea Ridge. Washington sent him east to the Shenandoah Valley that spring, where he was bested by Stonewall Jackson like everyone else, then he led a corps in the defeat at Second Manassas in August. Sigel missed most of the action thereafter until he was assigned command of the Department of West Virginia early in 1864. Assigned to clear the Shenandoah, he conducted a hesitant and inept campaign that culminated in the Battle of New Market on May 14, when a numerically inferior Confederate army almost destroyed him. His men started chanting a new refrain, "I fights no more mit Sigel," and General Henry W. Halleck in Washington said that, "It is but little better than murder" to give commands to men like Sigel. He was soon relieved.

After the war Sigel lived another 37 years, moved to New York, and wrote several articles on his Civil War service, none of which removed the tarnish, but he always remained popular with the German-born soldiers who followed him. He died August 21, 1902.

A heroic bronze statue of him would be erected in New York City after his death. Like the general himself, however, it is tarnished and hollow.

EDMUND KIRBY SMITH

Critics often accused Jefferson Davis of being a tyrant and autocrat, but there was in fact one man in the Confederacy who was a virtual dictator, so pervasively powerful that a third of the would-be nation was sometimes called "Kirby Smithdom."

He was born Edmund Kirby Smith at St. Augustine, Florida, May 16, 1824, and in 1841 entered the Military Academy, where he finished in the bottom half of his class. He served under both Zachary Taylor and Winfield Scott in the war with Mexico, and afterward did brief frontier duty before taking a position as instructor of mathematics at West Point. Thereafter he served chiefly in Texas and the southwest until the coming of secession.

When Texas voted to secede in February 1861, Smith removed his small command of United States Regulars and was soon promoted to major, but in March he resigned his commission and entered the Confederate service as a lieutenant colonel. He first commanded a garrison at Lynchburg, Virginia, but in May joined the staff of General Joseph E. Johnston at Harpers Ferry. On June 17 he rose to brigadier general and command of a brigade that he took to the First Battle of Manassas with Johnston's army. Smith had just gotten off the train and led his men to the front when a bullet in the neck cut him down.

In October he rose to major general on his recovery, and led a small army in the ill-fated invasion of Kentucky in the fall of 1862. Then, despite the setback, he was promoted again, to lieutenant general and in January 1863 assigned command of the vast Trans-Mississippi department, virtually all of Texas, Arkansas, western Louisiana, and anything else the Confederates could occupy.

This was to be "Kirby Smithdom." Over the next two years, as the region became increasingly isolated from the rest of the Confederacy, Smith—now universally referred to as Kirby Smith to distinguish him from other Smiths—became not only military but also civil commander. Once the Mississippi was lost to the enemy, he ruled unchallenged, with another promotion to full general in February 1864. Generally unsuccessful as a field commander in the department, Smith still managed a civil administration that seemed almost impossible. He was among the last to give up, surrendering his paper thin army on June 2, 1865.

After the war, Kirby Smith engaged in failed business enterprises until he took the presidency of the University of Nashville, then moved to Sewanee to teach at the University of the South. When he died March 28, 1893, he had outlived all the other seven full rank generals.

EDWIN M. STANTON

Lincoln regarded him as an almost indispensable weapon in forging victory, yet others thought him the president's enemy, and perhaps even his murderer.

Edwin McMasters Stanton contributed as much or more to Union victory as any other civilian except Lincoln himself, and yet few either liked or appreciated him. Born in Steubenville, Ohio, December 19, 1814, he was orphaned in his early teens and had to abandon school to support his family. He studied on his own instead, and later spent two years at Kenyon College, though he could not afford to finish a degree. He moved to Columbus and studied law, finally passing the bar in 1836.

His iron determination and application may have cost him his sense of humor, and made him dull and even unpleasant to be around, but they made him a success professionally. In 1849 he secured appointment as legal counsel for the state of Pennsylvania, holding the office until 1856, and at the same time attracting the attention of the state's leading politician, James Buchanan. Thereafter he rose to special attorney for the United States, prosecuting federal cases, and in 1860, when a vacancy occurred in President Buchanan's cabinet, he was appointed attorney general.

He had been a Democrat all his life, and when Buchanan left office Stanton left public life, but then in January 1862 Lincoln offered him an appointment as secretary of war, tribute to Stanton's reputation for honesty and efficiency. He accepted the position and brought order out of the chaos, inefficiency, and occasional corruption that had plagued the War Department until then. He was an able administrator and organizer, though Lincoln often had to intercede after Stanton's brusque manner offended a general or politician. Yet though the two were never intimate friends, they worked wonderfully together, and Stanton gave his president unswerving loyalty.

When Lincoln was assassinated, some fools then—and since—maintained that Stanton was implicated in the plot, but it was sheer nonsense. He continued to serve President Andrew Johnson, but they quickly fell out and Stanton was replaced in a move that precipitated Johnson's impeachment. Stanton remained a converted Republican, however, and accepted the offer of a seat on the Supreme Court when Grant was elected president. But Stanton was seriously ill. Just days after his appointment was confirmed, he died on Christmas eve 1869. Even then enemies invented the calumny that he died a suicide.

JAMES EWELL BROWN STUART

There were stories that he grew a beard to conceal a weak chin, rumors countered by his teenage nickname "Beauty." Certainly he stopped female hearts when he rode by in his black hip boots, wearing his plumed hat, and with his saber jangling, followed by that jolly and dashing retinue that included an enormous Prussian and a diminutive banjo player. By that time "Beauty" was long gone, replaced by a single syllable that was known universally, North and South...Jeb.

He was a Virginian, which alone won him many a heart. Born February 6, 1833, he was named James Ewell Brown Stuart to honor several family connections, and secured an appointment to the United States Military Academy, from which he graduated in 1854 with standing sufficient to gain a commission in the cavalry. From then until the outbreak of war he served mainly in frontier duty in Kansas facing Indians, and was wounded by an arrow in one hot skirmish. By sheer chance, he was in the east in October 1859, serving temporarily as aide to Colonel Robert E. Lee of the 2nd United States Cavalry, when they were ordered to put down the John Brown raid at Harpers Ferry. Stuart himself led the assault that finally broke into Brown's fort, and was one of the first inside.

Like Lee, Stuart chose to go with Virginia when she seceded, and immediately received command of the 1st Virginia Cavalry, which he led at the First Battle of Bull Run, a performance that won him promotion to brigadier general two months later. The early association with Lee paid off the next spring when Lee took command of the Army of Northern Virginia and he ordered Stuart to reconnoiter the Yankee army on the Peninsula. Stuart rode entirely around the enemy, gaining valuable intelligence and putting a fright into the always timid McClellan, and Lee rewarded him with command of all the army's cavalry, which Stuart would hold until his death.

He proved to be an almost ideal cavalryman, a team player who worked well within the chain of command despite occasional outbursts of adventuring. As a major general he harassed enemy armies, gathered vital intelligence for Lee, and created a legend of dash and daring. He helped win the Second Manassas Campaign, performed ably in the invasion of Maryland, and at Chancellorsville in May 1863 actually took command of the Second Corps after the wounding of Stonewall Jackson.

Stuart met his first real check at Brandy Station in June 1863, when he was surprised and almost defeated by Federal horse. In the Gettysburg Campaign he did not live up to Lee's expectations entirely, but the fault was as much Lee's as Stuart's. Certainly Lee never lost any confidence in the young cavalryman, and when Stuart was mortally wounded at Yellow Tavern on May 11, 1864, dying the next day, Lee was stunned, as was the Confederacy.

JAMES AND WILLIAM TERRILL

Heartbreaking as it must have been for any family to see its sons fight on different sides, there was one greater tragedy to suffer, and that was losing them both. It happened to few, but to none more tragically than the Terrills of Virginia.

The family lived in Bath County, which the boys' father represented in the state assembly for a number of years. William Rufus Terrill was born first, April 21, 1834, and his brother James Barbour Terrill (inset) followed a few years later on February 20, 1838. Both boys felt the attraction of the military, and their father managed to get William an appointment to West Point in 1849, and four years later he graduated ranking 16th in a class of 52. He spent the next eight years serving in the artillery in Florida, in Kansas, and teaching at the Military Academy. When the war broke out, he was a captain in the 5th United States Artillery.

With one son already in the Academy, the boys' father may not have been able to get James a similar appointment, or perhaps the boy wanted to stay closer to home. In any case, he entered the Virginia Military Institute at Lexington in 1854, graduating four years later, then studied law and had just set up his practice at home when the crisis came. Virginia's secession forced a decision on both of the Terrills, and perhaps their education either reflected—or influenced—their decisions. James cast his lot with the state that had trained him for the military. William, deeply divided between loyalty to home and to the United States that trained him, supposedly discussed his choice long and hard with his father, finally deciding he could not repudiate his oath to the Union so long as he did not have to serve in Virginia.

James Terrill won a commission as major of the 13th Virginia Infantry and fought at First Bull Run, and then in the Shenandoah under Stonewall Jackson, and on through all of Lee's battles to Chancellorsville. Promoted to colonel of his regiment, he led it at Gettysburg, the Wilderness, and Spotsylvania. On May 30, 1864, in the fighting at Bethesda Church, he was killed in action. Unbeknownst to him, his promotion to brigadier general was in the works, and was confirmed two days after his death.

As for William Terrill, he got his wish never to have to fight in Virginia. He started the war training recruits in Kentucky, then in 1862 became chief of artillery for the 2nd Division of the Army of the Ohio. He fought at Shiloh on the second day of the battle, and that fall resisted the Confederate invasion of Kentucky, after which he, too, was promoted to brigadier general, on September 9. He held his command of a brigade for just a month. On October 8, in the battle of Perryville, a shell fragment mortally wounded him. He died that night.

THE TEXAS BRIGADE

The new Confederacy stretched all the way from the Virginia coastline to the deserts of the New Mexico territory. The largest state in the young nation, as in the old Union, was Texas, itself once an independent republic. Most of the young men who enlisted in the Lone Star state stayed there during much of the war. The very first brigade to be raised, however, saw another destiny. It became known then and to posterity as the Texas Brigade, and in the Army of Northern Virginia it soon earned the sobriquet, "Lee's Grenadier Guard."

At the outset of the conflict several hundred men enlisted in a number of individual companies that were rushed east to Richmond soon after Virginia seceded, and the Confederate capital moved there from Montgomery. There they were organized into the 1st Texas Infantry and sent to the front in northern Virginia, to participate in the first Battle of Bull Run. Soon thereafter hundreds more men arrived, to compose the 4th and 5th Texas Infantries, and that fall they were brigaded with their predecessor and the 18th Georgia to form the Texas Brigade, the only one from their state to serve in the eastern theater. Commanded first by General Louis T. Wigfall, they would always be better associated with their most famous leader, General John B. Hood, and often called Hood's Texas Brigade.

They erected quarters at Camp Quantico in northern Virginia. It was their first war winter, and like all soldiers they erected such comfortable quarters as they could manage. The log huts of the Texans covered a wide area, a dozen or more men grouping together as a "mess" to build and occupy each cabin, and many of them were named for their officers and popular leaders. There was a Wigfall Mess, for instance, and here these two Texans pose before their Beauregard Mess, named for their army commander. Just which regiment these men belong to cannot be discerned, but the insignia of lone star and the word "TEXAS" atop the military kepi of the man on the right establish them as members of the brigade.

Soon enough whole cities of log winter huts like these would appear all across the continent, from Virginia to Missouri, the imagination used to make them homelike being truly inspiring. Some regiments even built glee clubs and theaters, one had a lending library, and not a few saw more feminine occupants as wives came to the camps to look after their husbands and their camp mates.

Ahead of them lay the Peninsular Campaign, the Seven Days, Second Bull Run, Antietam, Fredericksburg, Chancellorsville and Gettysburg, Chickamauga, the Wilderness and Petersburg, and Appomattox. No Confederate brigade earned greater fame and few saw wider service, a career in the inferno that belies the calm, almost jaunty appearance of two young Texans just on the edge of their time of trial.

GEORGE H. THOMAS

In an era of nicknames, his rang among the most dramatic. It all came from a September day in 1863, a day in which earlier he had almost panicked and played a role in bringing his army to disaster. But that afternoon he refused to move, and the Confederates could not go around him. That afternoon he became the Rock of Chickamauga.

Ironically he was a native Southerner, born to an old Virginian family on July 31, 1816. When he was 20, old for an entering cadet, George Henry Thomas was appointed to West Point, and finished in 1840 high in his class. His performance won him a commission in the artillery, and he stayed there until 1855, fighting in the Seminole conflict in Florida, and the war with Mexico where he won plaudits and promotion for daring. When the new elite 2nd United States Cavalry was created, Thomas got the plumb position of major, under Colonel Albert Sidney Johnston and Lieutenant Colonel Robert E. Lee, and served in the southwest until the coming of the Civil War.

Thomas bravely decided not to go with his native state when secession came, though it alienated his family from him for the rest of his life. He served first in the Shenandoah Valley, and in August got his general's star and transfer to Kentucky. There at Logan Crossroads, or Mill Springs, he won a small but significant early Union victory that helped collapse his old commander Johnston's Confederate line in Tennessee and Kentucky. He saw action on the second day at Shiloh on April 7, 1862, and won promotion to major general.

Thomas spent the rest of the war in the western theater, first as commander of a division at Perryville and Stones River, and later of a corps in the Army of the Cumberland. At Chickamauga heavy Confederate attacks at first nearly panicked him, and his repeated pleas for reinforcements weakened the center of the Union line just when the Confederates launched a crushing assault. With the army shattered and in retreat, Thomas stood for hours delaying the enemy pursuit, and winning his sobriquet. At Missionary Ridge in November he helped lift the siege of Chattanooga, and in the Atlanta Campaign to follow he commanded his army in Sherman's overall army group. At Franklin and Nashville, Tennessee, at the end of 1864, he all but destroyed the remnant of the Confederate Army of Tennessee in his last actions of the war.

Thomas enjoyed little of peacetime. He commanded in Tennessee during Reconstruction until 1867 and then was transferred to California, dying in San Francisco March 28, 1870. He still remains controversial, championed by some as an unappreciated genius.

Harriet Tubman

The people of the Civil War era were a generation highly influenced by their religion and the imagery of their Bible. They were all, on either side, convinced that they were doing their God's work. That applied to black as well as white, and in the emotionally charged atmosphere of freedom on the horizon, it was no wonder that biblical metaphors became common. Yet still there were surprises, and what more unusual than that it should be a woman that a people now called "Moses."

As was the case with so many one-time slaves, no one knew the exact date of birth of Harriet Tubman, though it was probably around 1821 in Dorchester County, Maryland. Certainly she was middle-aged by the time the Civil War erupted, and was herself an escaped slave who became an abolitionist of some note on attaining freedom in the North. In the decade before the war broke out, she repeatedly went into Maryland and Virginia and led groups of fugitive slaves back across the border to the North along the so-called "Underground Railroad." She was living in Auburn, New York, by 1861, already venerated as a symbol of the struggle for emancipation,

In early 1862, after Union forces had occupied party of the Sea Island area of coastal South Carolina, Massachusetts Governor John A. Andrew asked Tubman if she would go to Beaufort to help with the influx of runaway slaves—now called contrabands—coming into Union lines. Tubman spent the next several months in South Carolina, learning from the slaves the layout of the interior, and herself going behind Confederate lines both to scout the landscape, and also to help bring more slaves out. She did so with the aid and support of the military authorities, some of whom had already adopted the practice of hundreds of former fugitive slaves who called her Moses. She also nursed ill contrabands, and ran a small commissary selling things that she and they made to aid in their support while the military decided what to do with them.

In 1863 her role took a dramatic turn, as she started accompanying coastal expeditions. The first people the Yankees encountered were usually runaway slaves, and they would trust Harriet and tell her of Confederate forces and positions in the interior, which she relayed to the army commanders. In one expedition starting June 1, 1863, she actually planned and led the raid up the Combahee River that brought back more than 700 fugitive slaves. She remained at Beaufort until May 1864, meanwhile taking part in a raid on the Florida coast as well, and then returned home to New York, where she wrote a memoir, *Scenes in the Life of Harriet Tubman*, published in 1869, and reissued in 1886. The proceeds from the book, as well as most of what else she earned, she gave to black charities, and kept doing so until her death in March 1913, known universally as "the woman called Moses."

STAND WATIE

If anyone doubted that the Civil War was a thoroughly American affair, they had but to look west of the Mississippi, where not only whites and blacks, but also the native peoples, Hispanic and Indian, helped wage the war. One of them became the war's only Native American general.

Stand Watie, destined for future leadership in his tribe, was originally named Oowatie or Uweti at his birth in Rome, Georgia, December 12, 1806, but soon the family accepted the more phonetic spelling. They educated the boy at a mission school at Brainard, Georgia, but then sent him to Cornwall, Connecticut, for much more than the average Cherokee youth obtained in learning. Just as out of the ordinary, he was baptized into the white man's church as a Moravian. He became a planter in Georgia and helped his brother edit and publish the *Cherokee Phoenix*, the only native newspaper in the nation at that time. He was also active in tribal politics, and when the tragic removal of his people was forced by President Andrew Jackson in 1835, he yielded to circumstances and the next year helped lead his people to present-day Oklahoma. The Cherokee had been divided on accepting the removal, and reprisals brought the deaths of some who agreed like Watie to yield and emigrate, but he escaped to lead a large faction of Cherokees in their new homeland.

By 1861 Watie had become a prosperous planter and slaveowner, and took an early lead in trying to organize his people to side with the Confederacy and resist attempts at abolition. In June he raised a militia company, and two months later fought at Wilson's Creek, the first major battle west of the Mississippi. The Confederate authorities assiduously cultivated Indian alliances, and in October it commissioned him a colonel to form the Cherokee Mounted Rifles. Thereafter Watie often saw action, including the Battle of Pea Ridge in March 1862, but more often he operated as a partisan, raiding and gathering information. In June 1864 he even captured a Yankee warship on the Arkansas River, unaware as yet that the month before the Confederacy had commissioned him a brigadier general.

Several thousand natives of various tribes fought for the Confederacy, but most were loosely organized and difficult to control. Watie's strength was that he and his command almost always operated according to military practice, though even he was sometimes subject to the urge to settle old tribal feuds under the authority of his uniform. On June 23, 1865, the only Indian general of the war was also the last Confederate general to surrender. Afterward he returned to planting and tribal leadership, dying September 9, 1871, on Honey Creek in Oklahoma.

PICTURE CREDITS